THE
ADVENTUROUS
DECADE

THE ADVENTUROUS DECADE

Ron Goulart, 1933-

ARLINGTON HOUSE·PUBLISHERS
NEW ROCHELLE, NEW YORK

Copyright © 1975 Ron Goulart

Manufactured in the United States of America

Library of Congress Cataloging in Publication Data

Goulart, Ron, 1933-
    The adventurous decade.

    Includes index.
    1. Comic books, strips, etc.--United States--History
and criticism. 2. American newspapers--Sections.
columns, etc.--Comics. I. Title.
PN6725.G6   741.5   75-6725
ISBN 0-87000-252-X

Dedication
To William F. Nolan
Friend & Bibliographer

Contents

Preface

EVERYBODY KEEPS DOING the same book about comic strips. You always get the history from at least the Middle Ages on; sometimes they take you all the way back to the cave paintings at Altamira. This is inevitably followed by genuflections at the shrine of the *Yellow Kid* and a few kind words about Swinnerton's *Little Bears and Tigers,* a feature which never existed. It occurred to me that it was time to do a book about the funnies that didn't try to cover everything.

This book, as the title indicates, is limited to studying and giving the history of one specific type of newspaper strip. Even the adventure strip is a relatively vast topic, so I've concentrated on the 1930s, the decade in which *Flash Gordon, Terry and the Pirates, Dick Tracy,* the Sunday *Tarzan,* and sundry other adventure strips commenced. To understand the thirties, of course, you have to know something about the twenties. So we'll begin in the middle of the Jazz Age and follow the development and burgeoning of the straight-continuity strips through the depression and up to the brink of World War II.

I felt obliged to explore and discuss all the major features—*Buck Rogers, Captain Easy, Tarzan, Flash Gordon, Dick Tracy, Terry, Mandrake,* and *Prince Valiant,* for instance. But I've also devoted space to many of the lesser known, sometimes completely forgotten adventure strips of the 1930s. If, like me, you find the second bananas equally fascinating, you'll encounter a good many of them in the pages which follow: *Jim Hardy, Flyin' Jenny, Red Barry, Don Winslow, Scorchy Smith, Bronc Peeler, Radio Patrol, Speed Spaulding, The Red Knight, Charlie Chan, Frankie Doodle, Dickie Dare,* and *Myra North* . . . to name a few.

THE ADVENTUROUS DECADE

Chapter 1
What the...?

This book was begun and written while indestructible adventure strips were toppling. For some funny-paper heroes, the end was so swift there was hardly time to utter the favorite expletive of the adventure comics, "What the . . . ?" *Terry and the Pirates* collapsed, *Smilin' Jack* crashed, and *Little Orphan Annie* came tumbling after. *Terry* and *Smilin' Jack* both ended in early 1973, *Annie* held on a year longer and then went into reruns. Newspapers and magazines across the country ran thoughtful pieces about "the general decline of the serious adventure-serial comic strip." Many reasons for the decline and fall of the adventure strip were given. The favorite was competition from television. Then came the newsprint shortage and lack of space, changing social currents (AKA "the times they are a-changin'" explanation), and the fact that the quality of a good many of the straight strips had fallen off. The *New York Times,* always ready to clarify and put things in historical perspective, suggested that new humor strips like *Doonesbury* were supplanting the declining straights. "The 'joke strip' is actually a new generation of comic section art, perhaps best described as sophisticated funnies. It represents the third major development in the 82-year history of the comic strip in America."

13

I'd better warn you now that at the end of this book we won't arrive at any such all-encompassing explanation for what's happening to the adventure strip today. My purpose is not to explain major trends or to delve deeply into the sociological and psychological reasons behind them. I intend, simply, to talk about the many kinds of adventure strips that came to life in the 1930s and about the men who drew and wrote them. Which is not to say that you aren't free to draw your own conclusions about the more profound issues.

There are times when I admire writers who can begin a history with some line like: "On a crisp autumn morning in 1906, Charles W. Kahles seated himself at the drawing board and exclaimed, 'By golly, I think I'll invent the adventure strip today!'" Things are never that simple, though, and a great many different strands usually get woven together before anyone notices something new has been made. There were various precedents for the kind of adventure strip that flourished in the adventurous decade of the 1930s. Continuity had been a factor in comics practically from the start. Winsor McKay carried his stories over from Sunday to Sunday in *Little Nemo,* for instance. And long before the First World War, Harry Hershfield in *Desperate Desmond* and Kahles in *Hairbreadth Harry* were using continued stories. Their continuities, though, were mock heroic, parodying dime novels and melodramas. Somewhat closer to the mark was Tom McNamara, who was trying out boys-book continuities (one such involved being marooned on a desert island for weeks) in his *Us Boys* strip from about 1915 on.

Newspapers got seriously interested in continuing adventure stories at the same time the movies did. In fact, as Kenneth Macgowan pointed out in *Behind the Screen,* "the idea of serialization in print was basic to the first of America's true serials, *The Adventures of Kathlyn* (1913), and to many that followed. Week by week, the *Chicago Tribune* printed the plot of the current installment in order to draw new readers from the patrons of the nickelodeon." The Hearst papers adopted similar tactics. Serialized fiction, whether chopped up bestsellers or interminable romances written expressly for syndication, was a staple of newspapers when *The Perils of Pauline* and *The Hazards of Helen* hit the silent screen.

Edgar S. Wheelan also fell under the spell of the movies. A graduate of Cornell in the days when a cartoonist who'd been to college was something of a rarity, he'd been doing editorial cartoons and filler art on the *San Francisco Examiner* when Hearst summoned him East to work on the *New York American.* "Hearst had heard I

14

could draw just like Tad," Wheelan once told me. "What he really had in mind was to *scare* Tad into a ten-year contract, which he did by threatening to put *me* in *his* place. . . . It was a typical Hearst 'dirty trick.'" While with the *American* Ed Wheelan began to do a strip which ran across the top of one of the sports pages; "it had no name but burlesqued various films and stars of the silent era." This evolved into a larger strip he called *Midget Movies*. So far as I can determine, the first *Midget Movies* daily appeared on April 8, 1918. It was a one-day parody of a travelogue. The next two days were given over to a two-part continuity titled *The Heart of a Vampire*. Wheelan drew in a very electric and personal version of the big-foot style; his strips were all takeoffs on current films. This makes awarding him the title of Father of the Serious Adventure Strip a bit difficult, since he obviously wasn't serious. Not then, anyway.

Wheelan quit the *American* at the end of the decade. When alluding to his reasons in later years he was vague about specifics, but he implied they involved more of Hearst's dirty tricks. Signing up with George Mathew Adams's syndicate, he began doing his strip under the new title *Minute Movies*. Adams had risen in the syndicate business chiefly through the discovering and distributing of the poems of Edgar Guest, but he apparently had a sense of humor. Wheelan was allowed to keep kidding the hokum and sentimentality of the motion pictures. He introduced, gradually, a regular cast of characters. The first was Dick Dare, a pretty boy in the Hairbreadth Harry fashion. The epics, now running a week at least, were always directed by Art Hokum. Wheelan explained the sources of his characters this way: "Mary Pickford, when she wore long curls, was the one Hazel Dearie was patterned after, although at the time there was Grace Darling, Arline Pretty, Hazel Dawn, Louise Lovely, Bessie Love, and points west. Dick Dare was a combination of Francis X. Bushman and Wallace Reid, both blonds. Ralph McSneer was quite a composite of Lew Cody, Stuart Holmes, Lon Chaney, etc. Blanche Rouge was, of course, inspired by Theda Bara, with a touch of Carmel Myers. Fuller Phun was named during a corny era when such names as Fuller Bull, Fuller Pep, etc., were supposed to be screamingly funny; of course, Fatty Arbuckle was the model. . . . Paul Vogue was a poor excuse for Rudolph Valentino. Lotta Talent's piquant expression was lifted from Barbara LaMar (I hope I'm spelling these names right—it's been a long time). Will Power appeared by demand because I used him in so many 'pitchers' without credit, but I can't think of anybody who inspired the sharp-nosed sleuth."

NOTICE TO MINUTE MOVIE FANS

ON THIS SCREEN STARTING TO-MORROW WILL BE SHOWN THE GREATEST WESTERN PICTURE EVER FILMED. IN FACT, A SUPER-SERIAL DE LUXE WITH ALL THE WHEELAN MOVIE STARS ~~~~

THE MYSTERIOUS BANDIT.

DICK DARE TAKES THE PART OF A BOLD OUTLAW, BUT EVER READY TO AID A LADY IN DISTRESS ~~~

LOVELY HAZEL DEARIE AS "LITTLE NELL", THE OLD MINERS DAUGHTER GIVES A SUPERB PERFORMANCE

RALPH McSNEER AS THE GAMBLER HAS A ROLE THAT WILL MAKE HIM HISSED AND HATED THROUGHOUT THE LAND

STRIKING BLANCHE ROUGE SCORES A HIT AS THE SPANISH, DANCE-HALL GIRL

NO LOVER OF THE GOLDEN WEST CAN AFFORD TO MISS THIS SENSATIONAL FIVE-PART SERIAL, FULL OF THE ROMANCE AND GLAMOR OF THE OLD MINING DAYS! THRILLS - EXCITEMENT - LOVE MYSTERY AND LOTS OF OTHER THINGS!!

Remember fans - it starts Here To-morrow!

Like the movie studios, Ed Wheelan announced his coming attractions, as in this strip from the early 1920s. It also saved him a day of plotting. © George Mathew Adams.

Using the motion pictures as a taking-off point, Wheelan put his actors into every kind of story. He utilized long shots, close-ups, and other camera-inspired setups. As the 1920s progressed his continuities grew longer, taking up three or four weeks. In between he ran mock newsreels, animated cartoons, and travelogues. Wheelan had a very strong awareness of his audience, and he frequently addressed them directly. He encouraged them to write in, to make scrapbooks of *Minute Movies* strips, to ask for advice. He devoted one or two strips each month to his "Answer Man" department, wherein he gave tips to aspiring cartoonists and writers who'd sent him samples. The Answer Man was a crusty old gent, as likely to tell you your drawings were awful as to hand out praise. To many of Wheelan's readers, his actors and actresses had become real. He frequently gave biographical information about his stars, kidding gossip columns but at the same time giving more life to the characters: "Dick Dare, popular leading man with 'Minute Movies,' having fallen in love plans to disregard his signed contract with the Wheelan forces"; "The new cafeteria recently opened on the Wheelan Lot proves very popular with the stars"; "During the hot weather Hazel Dearie decided to bob her hair." In the serials themselves Wheelan was able to try out every sort of format, and there's no type of later serious adventure strip he didn't use. There were cowboy continuities, airplane adventures, soldier-of-fortune yarns and, by the late twenties, when things were more serious, a series of detective stories with Will Power as Inspector Keene. In the Wheelan Pictures, Ink. movies, Dick Dare was inevitably the hero, appearing as Hal Fracas, Robert Rich, Bob Manley, Basil Sponge-Cake, Emery Stone, etc. Hazel was always the heroine, starring in such vehicles as *The Hazards of Hazel,* wherein she portrayed Hazel Knutt, "the cleverest lady-detective in all the East." Ralph McSneer, as might be expected, was rarely a good guy and showed up in such roles as Cyril Sinister, Sherwood Skamp, James Hound, Li Low, Sam Malice, and the Spider.

In 1929—it happened to a lot of real movie producers as well—Ed Wheelan got serious and arty. His stories became sentimental and sober; he began to adapt classics. His productions of *Ivanhoe, Treasure Island,* and other worthy properties built up his following among schoolteachers, but they changed the strip into something Wheelan once would have made fun of. He even, as all clowns are supposed to yearn to, did *Hamlet* (Dick Dare was Hamlet, Hazel Dearie was Ophelia, McSneer was Claudius). Wheelan may have sensed that

Two episodes from another early twenties Minute Movies *serial, in the days when Wheelan was nonserious. Doing the daily in two rows of panels meant twice as much drawing. Originally each row was supposed to*

be the size of a 35-mm film, and early strips had sprocket-holes drawn in.
© George Mathew Adams.

the public was in the mood for serious adventure. Another factor was the assistant he'd hired, a Russian named Nicholas Afonsky. Afonsky ghosted most of the classics adaptations; his work was stiffer, more sentimental, less comics-oriented. He stayed with Wheelan into the early 1930s. *Minute Movies*, which now had competition from as much as a whole page of new comics using straight continuity and film layouts, was dropping in popularity. Afonsky was hired away by King Features—another Hearst trick, Wheelan always believed. He replaced the Russian with Jess Fremon for a while, then in the last years did *Minute Movies* by himself again. When it ended he tried one more syndicated strip, a circus adventure called *Big Top*. The rise of the original-material comic books in the late 1930s provided him, as it did many other newspaper veterans, with a place to work. Wheelan drew numerous fillers for several publishers, and for *Flash Comics* he revived *Minute Movies*. Complete with the Answer Man.

Chicago seems to have been a font for continued stories of one kind or another. We saw the *Trib* using *The Adventures of Kathlyn*, and the radio soap opera would soon rise up there. In 1917 it was *The Gumps*. Drawn, if that's the word for it, by Sidney Smith, the Gump saga was conceived by Captain Joseph Medill Patterson. Patterson was a cousin of the *Tribune's* Colonel MacCormick. He founded the *New York News* in 1919 and was head of the Trib-News syndicate throughout his lifetime. Desiring a strip which would be "true to American life," Patterson had Smith draw chinless Andy Gump and his kin. *Gump* was a Patterson family word for nitwit, which indicates what the captain thought of the average man. The average man apparently agreed, since *The Gumps* was a massive success. Before his *Gump* period Robert Sidney Smith had done *Old Doc Yak*, a strip about goats. His people were slightly better looking. The daily *Gump* strip was usually static, with Andy and wife Min, and maybe rich Uncle Bim, sitting around and talking. They could talk for days on end: about domestic problems, social aspirations, and, of course, money. In panels which were two-thirds talk balloons, Andy would often search his soul: "How will I ever face the world after this? To be pointed out as a failure—The very ones who

———————————▶

A Gumps Sunday, from 1925, with just about everything—a desert island, a wild beast, gunplay, suspense, pathos, and Ching Chow at his aphoristic best. The introductory panel indicates that, despite all the copy, Smith and his crew meant the page for children. © 1925 The Chicago Tribune. Reprinted by permission.

20

SUNDAY NEWS

5 CENTS PAY NO MORE

Copyright 1925, by News Syndicate Co., Inc. Reg. U. S. Pat. Off.

NEW YORK'S PICTURE NEWSPAPER

5 CENTS PAY NO MORE

Comic Section   New York, Sunday, MARCH 15, 1925.   Published Each Sunday   5 Cents   Everywhere in the United States and Canada

fawned on me for favors will be the first to mock and jeer. It seems unjust that one false step should blacken a man's good reputation forever. I'm a strong man. I can begin life anew but my heart aches when I think of Min and little Chester. Instead of riches and luxury I offer them disgrace and poverty. If I had only listened to Min's wise words. She warned me against trusting that swindler, J. Ambrose Hepwing." All this somehow charmed a vast public, the countrywide demand for *The Gumps* built the Trib-News syndicate. In the 1920s the continued stories, such as the one in which Uncle Bim almost married the Widow Zander, were matters of national concern. Amos 'n Andy, using similar suspense tricks, did the same thing on the radio in the thirties. Smith made an enormous amount of money out of his strip. He signed the first $1,000,000 contract ever given for a comic strip, getting it in yearly chunks of $100,000. He bought a Rolls Royce, an estate or two, and clothes. "He was a muscular guy and dressed in the height of fashion," recalls Will Gould about a visit to Smith's summer place in Wisconsin. "But he had a peculiar Fetish: he liked to wear his clothes tight to show off his bulging biceps and calf muscles. . . . On the beautiful lawn just off the lake was a $35,000 bronze statue of Andy Gump." Gould dropped in on Smith in the company of Brandon Walsh, who was writing continuities for *The Gumps* in the twenties. Sidney Smith had had a variety of people helping out. Sol Hess, a jeweler by profession, wrote gags and continuities for him until he started his own typical family strip, *The Nebbs*. Harold Gray was an assistant before going into the waif business.

During Walsh's stint with the Gump clan, the Sunday page was frequently taken up with the adventures of Andy's son, Chester. The things that befell the lad had a strange daydream quality. Uncle Bim would summon little Chester off to some remote place and the fun would begin. Unlike some later funny-paper moppets, Chester was a well-behaved and polite kid. What is more, almost everybody he met liked him. "Wouldn't you like to be little Chester traveling on such a wonderful train to visit his rich Uncle Bim? When he reaches Australia he will have the most marvelous toys and he will live in a great big beautiful castle like a little prince." On a later jaunt to Australia, this one by blimp, Chester gets marooned on a Pacific

———————————▶

Junior Nebb, a sort of spinoff of Chester Gump, led a fairly eventful life in The Nebbs *Sunday pages.* © 1937 Bell Syndicate, Inc. Reprinted by permission.

22

THE NEBBS

Junior Takes a Bad Spill

By SOL HESS

island with Uncle Bim's servant, Ching Chow. Ching Chow, who later got a panel of his own, is the first of many epigrammatic Chinese who will inhabit adventure strips. "It is written that every rope has two ends. . . . It is written that patience and a mulberry leaf will make a silk gown. . . . It is written when heaven has endowed a fool at his birth it is a waste of instruction to teach. . . ." The influence of Smith's strip and the variations of those who worked with him will be showing up in later chapters.

Others strips of the 1920s which established patterns that would be followed by a multitude of adventurers in the 1930s were *Tarzan* and *Wash Tubbs*. Each of them will have a chapter of its own.

Chapter 2
Lickety Whop!

REVOLUTIONS DON'T ALL start in the same way. Some of them begin quietly and unobtrusively. It's only after one of these bowls you over that you realize it had been inexorably rolling toward you for quite a while. The strip that was a major contributor both to ending the domination of the joke-a-day feature and to the explosion of adventure strips in the thirties began quietly and unobtrusively in 1924 under the title *Washington Tubbs II*. The work of a twenty-two-year-old Texas boy named Roy Crane, it took a while to get going. Crane wasn't even sure at first of what kind of strip he was doing. Once he found out for himself, there was no stopping him. He began to write and draw like nobody before. There was an ease and grace to his stuff, an admirable pace. He mixed action, humor, and romance. There were pretty girls, brawls, chases, sound effects. It was like the movies.

Royston C. Crane was born in Abilene, Texas, in 1901. He grew up in Sweetwater, a small town forty miles west of Abilene. His father was an attorney, and Crane was an only child. "My son says he became interested in art largely because he was a lonesome kid," his father recalled after Crane had started doing *Wash Tubbs*. "Roy had no brothers or sisters and he had to entertain himself. His mother and I, from the time he was a very small boy, would set him on the floor with picture books and magazines, scratch tablet and pencil and go about our business. By the time he was ten he was drawing comic strips." When Crane was fourteen he signed up for C. N. Landon's mail-order cartooning course. This was to have a major influence on his life. By 1924 Landon was also art editor for the NEA syndicate. "My early investment of $25 in the Landon course paid off," says Crane. But he had several years to fill between taking the correspondence-school lessons and starting the *Tubbs* strip.

In his high school years Crane worked at odd jobs his father found for him and as a soda jerk in a Sweetwater drugstore. He kept at his drawing. "I proposed doing an illustrated diary and received 50¢ a week from my father for it." Crane's drawing was pretty scratchy at this time, his lettering bad. He had trouble drawing girls at all. "I wish I could draw 'em," he commented under one inept sketch in his pictorial diary. As Crane remembers it, many of his part-time jobs didn't last long. "When I was sixteen years old I cut short a visit to Dallas to return to Sweetwater where my father had gotten me a job jerking soda. I was fired after a week." Celebrity being what it is, and small towns being what they are, that same drugstore took out a full-page ad congratulating Crane when *Wash Tubbs* began running in the local paper in 1930.

In 1920 Crane, like a good many other cartoonists we'll be encountering, went to Chicago to study at the Academy of Fine Arts. He stayed there six months. Among his instructors was Carl Ed, who'd started *Harold Teen* for the Chicago Tribune Syndicate the year before. One of Crane's assignments was to do a comic strip. He called his *Hash & Topsy*, and it was, significantly enough, about a brash young man who was looking for quick riches. Ed gave him a grade of Excellent. After his spell in Chicago, Crane returned to Texas. He worked on a couple of newspapers, dropped out of a couple of colleges. Wanderlust hit him hard about this time. When the dean of the University of Texas ruled that "Roy Crane is not by any stretch of the imagination qualified to remain as a student," Crane took off. As Crane put it, "When the bottom of my swimming lake blew away in a cloud of dust, I caught a freighter and went to sea." A lot of dissatisfied and restless college boys have made low-budget grand tours the same way. Crane got something extra out of his wanderings, experiences which would later become *Wash Tubbs* and *Captain Easy*.

Crane served as a seaman on the freighter, got stranded in Antwerp when he returned late from shore leave. He caught up with his ship in Wales, just in time to ride through a storm at sea which nearly sundered the craft. When he arrived in New York City he decided to try for another newspaper job. He was hired by the *New York World*, where he did staff art and also worked as assistant to H. T. Webster. Helping out on Webster's panels may have inspired Crane to try a panel of his own. At any rate, he eventually came up with a panel entitled *Music to the Ear*, with gags built around *Ain't It a Grand and Glorious Feeling?* sort of situations. United Features signed him up. Then tried to sell the panel. Only two papers bought it, meaning Crane and the syndicate would have been splitting a total take of $2 a week. The syndicate told Crane he might be able to unload the thing on another United Press operation, NEA. And that put Crane in contact with his former mail-order mentor, C. N. Landon.

Landon wasn't interested in a panel, but he asked his former pupil to try a comic strip. So Crane did. The strip, under the title *Washington Tubbs II*, began running in the early months of 1924. It was originally intended as a gag strip with simple, if any, continuity. "The funny situations worked out by Crane," explained the promo-

Washington Tubbs II in the brief pre-adventure phase of his career. © 1924 *NEA. Reprinted by permission.*

tion copy, "bring in Wash's employer, the owner of a grocery store, and Dotty Dimple of the movies, who is Wash's best girl. Of course there is a rival which leads to amusing complications." These amusing complications did not always readily occur to young Roy Crane, and he was soon unhappy with the way the strip was going. I got the impression when interviewing him that even now, a half-century later, he is still somewhat puzzled as to why Landon bought *Wash Tubbs* in the first place. NEA already had a successful funny strip with a general-store background in George Swanson's *Salesman Sam*. There was even another Wash, the Negro cook in J. R. Williams's cowboy panels. Perhaps Landon, like the old fortune-teller Wash Tubbs was soon to encounter, had the power to see into the future. Perhaps he had some premonition of what Crane would turn the strip into over the next few years. There wasn't much to recommend *Washington Tubbs II* in its first weeks. The comedy was thin, the drawing clumsy and ill-at-ease. Even Dotty Dimple of the movies wasn't much to look at.

Fortunately Crane remained dissatisfied. The strip had started running before he'd really thought out what he was going to do with it. He didn't feel he was particularly good at thinking up jokes. "The problem was what the hell to do . . . ideas like DeBeck or *The Gumps* or what?" Working at the NEA offices in unromantic Cleveland, Roy Crane dreamed of adventures in faraway places. "I wanted to be a hell of a long way off," he told me. "About the furthest off I could think of was the South Seas." Since Crane wasn't able to go himself, he sent Wash Tubbs. He worked up to the departure gradually. Toward the end of June 1924, Wash wanders into a fortuneteller's. He wants to find out how he's going to do with Dottie. The old crone, however, has other things to tell him. ". . . I see sunken ships—troubled waters—a strange man giving you a paper he doesn't wish to part with. Beware! There is another strange man! He smells of salt and distant lands—I see a dagger and but one eye—" A few days later an odd old seaman does give Wash a paper, but it doesn't seem to mean anything. And a burly sea captain begins to watch him. His name is Caliente Tamallo, and he's a rough forerunner of that quintessential rowdy, Bull Dawson.

One of Crane's favorite books was *Treasure Island*, and this first real adventure of Wash's was inspired by it. In the middle of August Wash suddenly disappears. He shows up a week later in San Francisco, having, like Crane in his youth, ridden the rods. He's figured out that the mysterious paper is a treasure map. He writes to his

28

boss at the general store, "Me for th' great open spaces where men are men and boys will be boys. Yours for BURIED TREASURE and lots of it." Wash joins the crew of a freighter which will take him to Australia. From there he plans to get somehow to the South Sea island he seeks. "Before him lies romance! Adventure!" announces a caption. "And possibly dissillusionment. Who knows?"

Wash is shipwrecked before he reaches Australia. He is marooned on a desert island, which turns out to be the very island he was looking for. It is populated with sarong-wearing natives—cartoony men and pretty girls. Better at drawing women now, Crane began here to clutter his strips with the cute girls that became one of his trademarks. Tamallo, the sinister sea captain, shows up on the island. Wash triumphs over him, finds the buried treasure, and returns home to "strut his stuff." This is the first of Wash's rise to great riches, each of which will always be followed by a tumble back down to rags. In the first months of 1925 Wash again courts Dottie. He also gets fleeced by a bogus count with a money machine. The count is the first in a long line of swindlers and con men who will take advantage of Wash. Crane, and his successor, Leslie Turner, were extremely fond of pretenders, imposters, and bunco artists.

The Wash Tubbs who begins to emerge in the strips is very much a 1920s hero. The sort of character, for instance, that Harold Lloyd had been developing in his comedy films since the early twenties, the "eager and bumbling young man" who is determined to succeed. The go-getter. He may be either timid or brash, but he is always likable. Wash Tubbs was certainly a go-getter, an optimist who believed in his own inevitable success. Crane often showed him, in the strip's first months, loafing around the grocery store studying a book titled *How to Get Rich*. Although Wash has moments when he feels "it's always me that's th' goat," he is also certain that "if I just had a chance I know I'd amount to something some day!" Crane knew what he was doing now. He abandoned the gags and the grocery store to concentrate on adventure.

Over the next two years Wash got involved in both foreign and domestic adventure. He acquired a new girlfriend, a brunette named Roxie, and got himself a sidekick. In the fall of 1926 Wash is marooned again, which leads to his meeting Gozy Gallup. Gozy is a slick, mustached young man who shares Wash's interest in action, get-rich-quick ideas, and dimpled girls. But he's not much better in a fight than the not quite five-foot-tall Wash. Teaming up with Gozy, Wash rambles round the world. They court a set of twins in Wash's hometown, work at a girls' school, and then join a circus wherein Wash falls under the spell of a tough lady tiger-tamer named Tango. Crane, who had himself briefly joined a traveling circus during his college-year wanderings, continued to be fascinated with the aggressive tomboy type of girl he first used in this sequence. He never grew tired of tigers either, introducing them frequently over the years and in some unlikely places.

After their circus stint Wash and Gozy tangle with bandits in Mexico and then, while on another island treasure hunt, they meet Bull Dawson. Dawson, the thick-necked and lowbrowed sea captain, is the prince of rotten guys. He is vicious, brutal, cunning, and hypocritical. He swaggers, scowls, smashes. He picks on people smaller than himself, especially Wash, and when he punches them a BAM! sound is heard. To the rowdy Dawson everybody is a softie. He is boastful, too. While successfully beating up both Gozy and Wash, he says, "Ain't never seen the day I couldn't handle the likes o' you pretties by the boatload an' call it fun." He urges his villainous crew to action with cries such as, "Man the boat, me bully boys!" Though Wash and Gozy win out in their 1928 encounter, it is obvious that Bull Dawson is going to return someday. He's going to beat up Wash again, too, unless someone a lot tougher than Gozy takes his side. Someone, say, like Captain Easy.

It was the resolution of a desert sequence in the fall of 1928 which led to the creation of Easy. Wash and Gozy go up against the sinister Hudson Bey in order to save Princess Jada. When the two men are lost in the vast Sahara, a black harem slave named Bola finds them. Later Bola helps them overcome Hudson Bey. Then, when Wash and Gozy fall into the hands of Sheik Bumfellah, it is Bola once more who rides off to return with a whole flock of French colonial troops. Crane explained to me that his brother-in-law had kidded him about this particular sequence. "He told me you shouldn't have a eunuch save them," Crane recalled. "What you need is a two-fisted guy." He had been thinking about the character of Wash Tubbs for some time. Crane felt Wash was an underdog, somewhat like Jim Hawkins in *Treasure Island,* who "obviously had a hell of a time taking care of himself." He had these things in mind when his brother-in-law made his criticism. A few months later Crane introduced Easy to the strip. When I mentioned that the Easy of those days looked something like Tom Mix and asked Crane if he'd had the cowboy star in mind, he replied, "No . . . since this brother-in-law of mine had suggested it, I used him as a model." Easy is not a Texan like Crane, but "a Southern gentleman." He almost didn't get named

Easy. "I was thinking of a name for him while walking from the studio up to get a streetcar," Crane said. "And I thought of his name, but I didn't have anything to write it down with." By the time he got around to writing the name down, Crane wasn't sure he remembered it correctly. He put down Easy, but now "I believe it was Early." Easy or Early, the captain was about to run away with the *Wash Tubbs* strip.

The advent of Easy. He was a lot uglier, and tougher, then. © *1929 NEA. Reprinted by permission.*

In December of 1928 Wash journeyed to the tiny kingdom of Kandelabra. What with one thing and another ("He finds that Jada, a girl he once befriended in the Sahara, is in reality a princess and rightful heiress to the throne. The Grand Vizer of Kandelabra is a crook. Not only that, but he hopes to make himself king by marrying Jada and deposing goofy King Goober"), by the spring of 1929 Wash is locked up in the dungeon of an ancient fortress known as the Black Castle. "Tubbs evidently left to die," Crane tells his readers in the headline style he then was using on captions. "Ingenious device fires pistol at him as he opens door. Fears other three doors are deadly traps also." Eventually Wash does get out of his cell, but he can't find his way out of the haunted castle. "Wash wanders thru castle . . . Seeks way out after numerous close calls." Then, on the fateful day of May 6, 1929, while revolution rages outside, Wash comes upon yet another oaken door. He commences tugging on it. A hook-nosed, unshaven man looks out through the barred window in the door. "What in blazes you up to—trying to get in here?" he snarls. "Dang foolishness, says I. I been trying to get out for months." It is Easy, and from now on, though he and Crane don't suspect it yet, Wash is going to be second banana.

Wash locates a crowbar and gets to work on the imprisoned Easy's door, asking, "American, aren't you?" "Well, yes and no," Easy replies. "Started out that way. Hang my hat on any old flagpole now. Like a flea, I reckon—most any old dog looks like home-sweet-home to me." Borrowing the crowbar, Easy breaks down the door himself. As he dusts his hands off, Wash says, "My name's Wash Tubbs—G. Washington Tubbs. Wot's yours?" "Easy. Just call me Easy." He leads Wash to a secret exit he knows about. "Er—wot'd you say your last name was?" Easy answers, "Don't recollect, suh, as I mentioned my last name." "Wow!" thinks Wash. "A hard-boiled bozo!"

The two new acquaintances have to fight their way out of the dungeon. "Down goes the navy as Admiral Tubbs is overcome by avalanche of blows, but 'Easy' proves to be master brawler and whips three with ease." Noticing Tubbs's plight, Easy remarks, "Blazes! Looks like my runt pardner isn't doing so well." With a smashing punch he takes care of Wash's antagonist. After the brawl Wash is enthusiastic. "Oboy! Wotta scrapper! Why, you're the best I ever saw." Easy says, "Lucky I'm good then. You're terrible. Thought you said you could fight! Blazes! You couldn't lick a postage stamp. That little runt hit you so many times he . . . Why, what's the matter? Hurt your feelings, didn't I? Aw, kid, I'm sorry . . . you're O.K., son—a game kid. Bum fighter maybe, but dead game." It is the beginning of a nearly half-century friendship.

Easy, it turns out, has also been working for Jada. He's been posing as a captain of artillery, and the princess is the first one in the strip to call him Captain Easy. Actually, Easy has been serving as chief of the Kandelabran Intelligence Service. "Well, dern my sox!" exclaims Wash when he hears this. "So you're a detective!" After ending the country's civil war and putting Jada on the throne, Wash and Easy refuse high positions in her kingdom and slip quietly out of the country. After a few days in Paris the new team catches "the first boat for the USA." Back in his hometown, with Easy as his guest, Wash gets embroiled with a phony countess and finally comes to be the prime suspect in a murder case. Easy, using both his detective abilities and his fists, sets out to clear his friend. At one point the police detective, suspicious of Easy, asks him, "What's your full name? Where's your home?" "Known gen'rally as just Easy, suh. Captain Easy," he answers. "Hum! Your occupation?" "Beach-comber, boxer, cook, aviator, seaman, explorer, and soldier of artillery, infantry and cavalry, suh."

Bull Dawson, supposedly living an honest life in Wash's very hometown, recurs in the strip now. Just before Christmas of 1929, Easy and Dawson tangle for the first time. Easy suspects Dawson is mixed up in the murder, and while watching his hideout he's jumped by the big rowdy. Fighting foul, as usual, Dawson whacks Easy over the head with a board, telling him, "Ain't never seen the day I couldn't whip the likes o' you in carload lots." When Easy returns home and Wash asks what happened, he answers, "Got heck beat out of me. Dawson caught me." "I betcha old Bull don't look like any chorus boy hisself." "All he got was some skinned knuckles, that's what." "Well, did you find out anything . . . ?" "All I found out, laddie, is that Bull Dawson is one tough baby." Already Captain Easy is somewhat more complex a character than the average two-fisted hero of pulps and silent movies. He doesn't always win. Nor is he always right. It turns out both he and the police are wrong about the murder. The deathbed confession of the spurious countess is what finally gets Wash off free.

Easy and Wash stick together for all of 1930 and part of 1931, getting dumped on an island by Bull Dawson, outwitting headhunters, becoming mixed up in a revolution in the Central American country of Costa Grande. In this latter sequence the team makes one of their earliest mutual quick climbs to fabulous wealth. They help an

The ORIGINAL
IS STILl

TREASURE ISLE AND THE LURE
OF PIRATE GOLD

AL

AN INTRIGUING PLOT —
AND SUSPENSE ON THE SAHARA

BUT BEFORE THE GRAND V
WASH GOES FOR A RIDE

DUELS AND ROM

VILLAINS
YOU LOVE
TO HATE

CLIPPI
PAST
EXPLAI
o
WAS

*Crane's syndicate began advertising the Tubbs saga as an adventure strip
from the late twenties on. Here's a trade ad from 1929.*

DVENTURE STRIP
THE BEST!

OVABLE HERO

CIRCUS
LIFE—
AND
LOVE

B'LIEVE ME, THAT'S ONE BRAVE GIRL, WASH.

W THE FINISHING TOUCH,
UNDING ATMOSPHERE.

N TINY KANDELABRA

PRETTY GIRLS
AS ONLY CRANE
CAN DRAW
THEM!

FROM
RIPS
OPULARITY

TUBBS

YO HO! YO HO! GATHER 'ROUND AND SEE THE MAR-VE-LOUS FEATS OF MAGIC, THE—

DR. DU
MEDICINE
SHOW

FUN WITH A MEDICINE SHOW

ZIP

BANDITS!

ACTION—
THRILLS IN MEXICO

eccentric scientist sell a bomb-exploding device to the ruling party. "The Americans become the richest men in Central America. The invention is SOLD! One hundred and fifty million dollars is there!" Crane, characteristically, has the money paid to them in small bills stuffed in huge sacks with dollar signs emblazoned on the sides. And, also characteristically, the invention proves to be a fake and the money counterfeit.

In the summer of 1931 Crane decided to tell something about Easy's past. He revealed that Captain Easy's real name was William Lee. Easy was a West Point man and had been married. Now there appears, at least to Wash, to be a possibility of Easy's clearing his name and remarrying ex-wife Louise. So Wash writes his partner a note and takes off alone. "Well old pal, by the time you get this I guess I'll be on my way. . . . I never expected to see you marry some bon bon. I always thought you would get shot. Well I never guessed that your dad ever ran for the U.S.A. senate either—I always thought you were a bum like me because you never comb your hair I guess. Do not try to find me, I am doing what is best for your own good as I would only get you in scrapes again. Best wishes, your old pal, Washington Tubbs." Apparently Crane later wished he had kept Easy a man of mystery. "Crane said afterwards he was sorry he had revealed this about Easy," reports an NEA contemporary, "but he did it in a moment of weakness. However, Easy extracted a promise from Wash never to bring up the subject again and it was never mentioned in the strip since."

Tubbs travels away from Easy by way of freight train and truck tailgate. He has a few solo adventures, then teams up with a ski-nosed tough guy named Rip O'Day, who looks something like Buz Sawyer's Roscoe Sweeney will look. O'Day is more a sidekick type. He's not a hero, certainly not another Easy. The public, Roy Crane himself, and, more importantly, several newspaper editors around the country missed the hook-nosed captain. Easy returns in the spring of 1932, wearing a mask and calling himself the Asiatic Monster. He and O'Day get into a fight, which stretches over several days' strips. Easy wins, and Wash's eyes light up. "There never was but one fella could fight like him—an' 'at's old EASY. C'mon, I know you!" O'Day fades from the strip, and Easy and Wash become partners for good. Later that year, after escaping from a prison island, they get involved in another revolution. "Ex-convicts leap from hoosegow to army commands! Become big shots overnight! Pockets are lined with gold, and fame and fortune beckon." This rags to

36

riches to rags to riches formula, frequently unfolding against a mythical light-opera-kingdom background, continued through the early and middle 1930s. "I loved those little countries," Crane told me. The war, however, was coming closer, and everything, even comic strips, was going to change.

Before we follow the Tubbs and Easy team into the real war, we'll back up in time a few years to take a look at Crane's Sunday pages. The *Wash Tubbs* Sunday began in 1929 and was, befittingly enough, small. It occupied one-third of a page above the two-thirds devoted to J. R. Williams's *Out Our Way* characters. Really this was little more than a four-color daily, with no continuity and a gag payoff each week. NEA had been talking with Crane for some time about doing a Sunday page of some sort. Early thinking had favored a completely different feature, and Crane had worked up at least two sample ideas, getting an okay for a full page that would deal with the Revolutionary War. The Crash of '29 postponed the debut of that one indefinitely. By 1933, when a full-page Sunday was again feasible, there was no doubt as to what it would be about—"We'd allowed Easy to run away with the strip"—and *Captain Easy, Soldier of Fortune* was brought forth. Easy was the absolute star of the Sundays; Wash wasn't even allowed in them for several years. The opening sequence found Easy soldiering as a pilot in the Chinese air corps. He next crossed swords with a tyranical Eastern mogul (finding time while a captive of the mogul to wrestle with a tiger, and tie a knot in its tail), outwitted a gang of Chinese pirates, hunted for treasure in a sunken city, and generally had a fine time. These early Sundays stimulated Crane, and he put some of his best work into them. Since nobody had to worry about chopping the pages into various sizes in those innocent, uncommercial days, Crane could do anything he wanted in his full pages. Panels could be any size, depending on the story he was telling and the design he had in mind, and could run all the way across the page or all the way down one side. He was able to stage Easy's adventures much more flamboyantly in the Sunday format, to go in for much more in the way of backgrounds and action. Mountains, jungles, and eclectic palaces rose up, hordes of crazed warriors galloped across the scene, scores of harem girls lounged and languished. As Crane modestly puts it, "Doing the Sunday pages then was fun." It was in the Sundays, too, that he developed and expanded his use of sound effects. Huge BAMS accompanied explosions, YEOWS of pain decorated brawls, punches produced the sound LICKETY WHOP! While Easy is escaping, on ele-

Easy and the pirates. One of Roy Crane's early Sunday pages, complete with sound effects and pretty girl. © 1934 NEA. Reprinted by permission.

phant-back, with a rescued harem girl, the native drums begin sending signals. Quietly at first—bum bidy bum—but soon growing louder and more ominous—Diby Daby Dum! Dum! DUM! DUM!

Roy Crane was soon devoting most of his time to turning out the *Easy* Sunday. This meant taking on extra hands. The erratic quality of the 1930s dailies is due to the trying out of several assistants and ghosts, chief among them being Bela Zaboly. Crane was relatively satisfied with him, but NEA liked Zaboly's work, too, and gave him the *Major Hoople* panel when Gene Ahearn was lured away to King Features. Soon after that Crane asked his old friend Leslie Turner to help out for a while. Although fonder of the lighter kind of adventure sequences, Turner had the job of handling the increasingly serious *Wash Tubbs* dailies while Crane continued with the *Captain Easy* Sundays. The Sunday sequences became more and more screwball toward the end of the thirties (it was in a weekend story that Crane introduced the magical animal known as a swink). "When the war came along we switched to pretty serious stories," Crane recalls. "And that demanded serious drawing." Except on Sunday.

Leslie Turner has described his life and career this way. "When Crane left in 1943 I inherited the strip. . . . This chore has left little time for anything eventful." He'd been Crane's assistant and frequent ghost for several years before the strip officially passed into his hands. "In 1937 I pinch-hit for Roy Crane on *Wash Tubbs* while he frolicked in Europe," he explains. "Stayed on as assistant till he left for greener pastures." Crane had apparently thought Turner would come along to those greener King Features pastures with him. "I left NEA to do *Buz Sawyer* . . . expecting Les to go with me. But NEA grabbed him," Crane says. "And there I was . . . new strip, daily and Sunday, middle of the war, and absolutely nobody available who could give me any real help." Crane's switch to King came as pretty much of a surprise to Leslie Turner. He told me he hadn't given much consideration to carrying on *Wash Tubbs* on his own, but when the offer to take over came from NEA he accepted without hesitation. The friendship between the two men, which dates back further than that of Easy and Tubbs, survived that wartime strain. Crane eventually found not one new assistant, but several. Turner stuck with Easy for another quarter-century, quitting late in 1969, a few weeks before his seventieth birthday. He passed the strip, which had been called *Captain Easy* both daily and Sunday since 1949, over to his assistant.

Turner was born in Cisco, Texas, "in time to see the last week of the nineteenth century." He grew up in Wichita Falls, almost com-

Pow! • Europe a Living Comic Stri

Here's a trip to Europe with a famous comic artist, all in one panel of pictures. Artist Roy Crane, whose pen traces the adventures of Wash Tubb and Cap'n Easy in The News, is just back from an extended tour. He found plenty of old-world color, and also managed to blunder into a Wash Tubbsian situation himself aboard ship, a situation his pen recorded in the sketch at lower right.

When Crane traveled to Europe in 1937, things still had a light-opera look to him. That would soon change.

pleted four years at Southern Methodist University, spent part of a term at the Chicago Academy of Fine Arts. It was in Chicago at the academy that Turner first met his fellow Texan Roy Crane. Like Crane he suffered from wanderlust in his youth and devoted his summers to riding the rods. This fondness for trains stayed with Turner and, even though he no longer traveled under them, he often built Tubbs and Easy adventures around trains. His first professional job after drifting out of college was in a Dallas engraving plant. At the same time he was sending cartoons in to *Judge*, and selling a few. After marrying in 1923, he and his new wife headed East. In New York Turner abandoned cartooning for illustration. He became a friend and pro-

40

tégé of the then prominent illustrator Henry Raleigh, and began doing work for *Redbook, Ladies' Home Journal,* and the *Saturday Evening Post.* Most of his illustrations were in a sober, realistic style with no trace of the lickety-whop! approach. Of course at this point, in the late 1920s, Turner had no idea he would someday be drawing a newspaper strip. What he was thinking about doing then was raising sheep. Since this was a short while before the stock market collapse, Turner perhaps sensed the need of a more dependable, down-to-earth job. He and his wife and daughters moved to Colorado. He stuck that out for three years, "drawing with one hand while rearing a herd of ungrateful sheep with the other." Finally, after another and less successful bout of freelancing in New York, Turner got the invitation from his longtime friend to come out to Cleveland and help out on *Wash Tubbs.*

"We each had our specialties," says Crane about the period when Turner assisted him. "I did the writing, drew all of the Sunday, all water and action on the daily, while he drew girls, aircraft, etc. The strip sprang back to life." At first Turner couldn't get the hang of his friend's style. He told me the most difficult thing was learning to draw with a pen again after years of using a brush. He gradually simplified his work, but for some time the energy and suppleness of the Crane approach eluded him. Turner did the daily while it was undergoing its transition from Ruritanian continuities to those involving more and more of what was going on in the real world. Easy went to work for the FBI, then got into the service. He quickly became a real captain, to avoid confusion. Wash, who'd married in the late 1930s, was less frequently seen. He stayed on the homefront working for his father-in-law, the grouchy tycoon J. P. McKee. Leslie Turner patiently rendered all the uniforms, gear, and weaponry required. What he really wanted to do, though, was comedy, and as soon as the Second World War ended he converted to a different kind of adventure.

Although Leslie Turner most often appears as a footnote to Crane in histories of the comics, he is really a very effective artist in his own right. By 1946 he had developed a strong style, built on some of the Roy Crane foundation blocks yet individual. He is the only artist to take over a major strip and equal, and sometimes surpass, his predecessor. Crane always worked fast; Turner derived much of his drawing enjoyment from a slower and more careful approach. An excellent figure and action man, he is equally good at backgrounds. His continuities are among the most convincingly placed in comics.

He can convey the look and feel of any location—a rundown English pub, a bleak stretch of southwestern desert, a brooding Victorian mansion. Turner also has a great eye for clutter, particularly lower-class clutter, which he details with as much loving care as George Price. Many of the foreign locales used in *Captain Easy* Turner didn't see first hand until after he retired, and for these he relied on scrap. For adventures unfolding in the United States he usually traveled to the spots he wanted to use. Turner enjoys traveling around the country by car, has often turned out his strips in hotel and motel rooms.

To match the new style of the postwar years, Turner came up with new characters and new kinds of continuity. For about the first year and a half of his tenure as artist, the scripts were written in NEA's Cleveland offices. Then Turner was allowed to do his own stories. From the Crane stock company he retained such as McKee, Bull Dawson, and Lulu Belle Suggs, "circus strong woman, wrestler, female boxing champ, holder of the world record in pig-lifting." He added several recurrent characters of his own, notably the Kallikak family. The Kallikaks are a vast and worthless clan of lowlifes, headed by Orville Kallikak and his wife and their nitwit son Buster. They have relatives everywhere in the world, anywhere that they might cause McKee, Wash, and Easy new trouble. Their name comes out of psychologist Henry Goddard's studies in heredity. His Kallikak family had two branches, one good and thriving, and the other composed of criminals, idiots, invalids, and paupers. Turner's Kallikaks all belong to this latter branch. When I talked to Turner recently he said the disreputable Kallikaks were among his favorite characters. Another favorite is Buckingham Ish, the prince of swindlers. Ish has only one mark: the bald, crotchety J. P. McKee. Like all successful con men, Ish always takes advantage of his victim's desire to make a quick buck by seemingly taking advantage of someone else. It is McKee's failing that he is always ready for one more get-rich-quick scheme, and never recognizes Ish in his latest disguise. The Ish type of clever scoundrel was one of the staples of popular fiction when Turner was growing up. He says remembrances of O. Henry's Gentle Grafter gave him the idea for the audacious Ish. From the late forties onward there were many episodes using the Kallikaks and Ish, plus satires on Hollywood, advertising, and contemporary life in general. Turner mixed these with straighter continuities about treasure-hunting and spy-catching. He now and then tried a serious continuity, such as one dealing with alcoholism. On this one he had a feeling the syndicate

Leslie Turner's version of the strip, four dailies from 1951. By this time he'd mastered all the Crane touches and added some of his own. In the first two samples the Kallikaks are again about to lead McKee astray. © 1951 NEA. Reprinted by permission.

might balk, so he sat on the drawings until it was too late to do anything else and then sent them in.

For nearly a decade Turner was only responsible for the daily. When Crane left NEA in 1943 they put the *Captain Easy* in the hands of Walt Scott. So unimaginative was Scott, then nearly fifty, that he'd spent most of his life until that time in Ohio, over twenty years of it working as a newspaper staff artist in Cleveland. Though Scott later showed a modest affinity for cute whimsy in a page called *The Little People*, he was completely unsuited to doing a Crane-style adventure strip. They let him stumble along with the *Easy* Sunday, though, until the summer of 1952. Then Turner took over. He was reluctant to add the page to his chores, but it meant more money and his wife persuaded him to try it. It says something for the vitality of Captain Easy that even nine long years of Walt Scott could not destroy him. The first Leslie Turner page appeared on August 31, 1952, in the middle of a Scott story. He began signing it two months later. The extra burden of a Sunday page apparently buoyed Turner up, at least initially, and the first two years contain some of his finest work. Turner exuberantly filled the page with sweeping desert scenes, idyllic shots of the New England seacoast, panoramas of English country estates and stately homes. It abounded with vintage automobiles, ocean liners, jets, and, of course, trains. Significantly, it was a little over six months after he added the Sunday to his work load that Turner did a weekend continuity with Wag Patakey, the deadline-missing cartoonist.

Patakey, who is a composite of Turner and Crane in looks, draws the famed strip *Giddy McWaddle*. When Easy first encounters him, through his lovely blonde daughter, the cartoonist is holed up in a deserted pueblo in a southwestern Indian village. Much the same as Turner, Patakey likes to travel around the country and is continually having to stop to bat out strips to meet the syndicate deadlines. Once he gets at the drawing board nothing can budge him until he is caught up. At the moment, the valley where he is working is about to be flooded by the opening of a new dam. As the water starts to rise, his daughter pleads, "We *must* get out of here before the new dam has this pueblo under water! For once you've *got* to miss a deadline!" "Never!" replies the weary-eyed cartoonist. "Move the car to the high ground and get a boat, or learn to swim . . . so you can get out to mail for me!" While Patakey slouches at his board, complaining, "I'm out of ideas! Six strips and a Sunday page every week for twenty-five years! Shakespeare didn't turn out that much!" The water continues to rise, and various vexations of a cartoonist's life are visited on him. The writer he's hired is no good; the syndicate doesn't believe his excuse for being late; the engravers are going to have two days off and the syndicate asks him to get even further ahead; a doting mother, traveling by rowboat, brings her son over for advice, saying, "He's awfully talented. . . . There ain't a billboard in the county he hasn't put a moustache on, Mr. Pattycake! An' any k·nd of *work* makes him sick! So if you'll show him how to be a cartoonist . . ." Finally, when the water is up to Patakey's waist, Easy carries him off and finds a way to help him get his drawings in on time. The cartoonist and his daughter invite Easy to stick around, but he replies, "Not *me!* Your racket is too nerve-wracking! I'll got dig up a bloodcurdling adventure, and relax!"

Turner stuck with the Sunday page for the remainder of the 1950s, alternating moderately blood-curdling adventures with broader farces starring Wash, McKee, Lulu Belle, the numerous Kallikaks, and Ish the swindler. After suffering a heart attack he had to give up the page. Mel Graff began ghosting the Sunday early in 1960, though Turner occasionally returned to do a page or two. The last of the Leslie Turner dailies ran in January of 1970; the final episode was about his old favorite, Buckingham Ish. Bill Crooks, assistant on the strip for nearly twenty-five years, assumed the drawing. Jim Lawrence, who'd scripted several humdrum strips previously, became the writer. When I talked to Leslie Turner late in 1974 he said he's been reading over a good many of his old proofs since he'd retired. The drawing, he felt, held up pretty well, but he thought the copy could have been a lot more concise.

Chapter 3
Tarzan Every Sunday

THE FIRST TIME they tried to sell *Tarzan* as a newspaper strip nobody bought it.

That was in 1928, when an advertising man named Joseph H. Neebe formed Famous Books and Plays Inc., to peddle a strip adaptation of *Tarzan of the Apes*. Neebe's adaptation was a sober-looking affair, with no rowdy balloons or sound effects. The Edgar Rice Burroughs prose was set in little blocks of type beneath the illustrations. This was not an innovation; syndicates had been doing that throughout the twenties with their short-run adaptations of such classics as *The Count of Monte Cristo* and *Pilgrim's Progress*. Neebe had been a Tarzan enthusiast since the ape man debuted in the pulpwood pages of *All-Story* in 1912; to him the Burroughs novel was also a classic. His first choice for artist was J. Allen St. John. The veteran illustrator had painted covers for several of the hardcover Tarzan novels, he'd even illustrated Balzac. But he and Neebe couldn't come to terms, probably because St. John had little faith in a funny-paper version of the Lord of the Jungle. Turning his back on illustrators, Neebe went next to a fellow advertising man, Harold R. Foster. "Joe Neebe had the idea for putting famous books and plays into newspaper comic strips," Foster recalls. "I'd done a lot of work for him as he was with an advertising agency I did work for, and he thought of me when he got this idea. He wanted to raise the tone of comics and Tarzan was the first."

Tarzan was by this time a formidable property. The novels, published by a company with the splendid name of McClurg, were immediate bestsellers. They were serialized in newspapers, translated into numerous foreign languages. The ape man became a movie hero in 1917, with chesty Elmo Lincoln portraying him. A comic strip should have been an automatic hit. "Neebe prepared very elaborate promotion and hired a staff of advertising salesmen to sell the feature to newspaper editors," said George A. Carlin, who was the general manager of United Features. "Apparently this approach of high-powered advertising salesmen was precisely what was not needed, because at the end of the campaign no newspapers had bought the feature." Neebe next went to the Metropolitan Newspaper Service syndicate and asked its owner, Maximillian Elser, Jr., to try and sell *Tarzan*. Before joining the syndicate in 1919, Elser'd done publicity for Pavlowa, Diaghileff, and the New York Philharmonic. So he had some experience with high-class things. His salesmen had better luck than Neebe's and sold the new strip to "a small but important list of newspapers." The first strip of the Neebe-Foster adaptation, which consisted of sixty dailies, appeared on January 7, 1929. When the sixty ran out, editors were to ask readers if they wanted to see further adventures of the ape man. The syndicate must have had a hunch they would, since their trade ads, as early as November 1928, were promising the first adaptation would be "followed by 10 others, each to run from 10 to 12 weeks." The reaction of course was favorable, but there was a problem. Hal Foster had returned to servicing his advertising accounts and didn't want to do any more funny-paper work. His last panel showed Tarzan kissing Jane's hand as he takes his leave. "Knowing he could have had Jane if he had told her of the proud name he bore, he still refused to do so. For Tarzan's pride was great. Sorrowfully he bids her farewell."

Fortunately there was another ex-advertising man handy, doing artwork right there in the Metropolitan bullpen. It was Rex Hayden Maxon of Lincoln, Nebraska—thirty-seven years old and well-intended, though no Hal Foster. From the eleventh week on, the jungle habitat was his. The new adaptation was of *The Return of Tarzan*. "A great ocean liner was nearing France. Aboard her was Tarzan of the Apes," says the copy under Maxon's first panel. "Think-

47

ing, rather sorrowfully, over the past few weeks, he wondered if he had acted wisely." So powerful is the basic idea of Tarzan that it gets through to the reader even through such sorrowful writing as this. And once Maxon gets Tarzan off the boat and into his leopard skin, the action picks up. In 1933 *Fortune* estimated the *Tarzan* strip was grossing $2,000 a week, of which Burroughs got about $1,200. This despite the fact that the "strip is even more inane than the famous Tarzan books." The Metropolitan had by this time merged with United Features. By the middle thirties United claimed over three hundred papers were carrying *Tarzan* daily and Sunday.

The Sunday page began in March 1931, with Rex Maxon doing the drawing. The impact of the newspaper *Tarzan* would have been far less if Maxon'd been able to keep up with the additional work of a Sunday. He wasn't, and Hal Foster was approached once more. The depression had arrived and taken hold since Foster's last spell of jungle fever. "I didn't think much of *Tarzan*, although a lot of people did," Foster has said. He took the job anyway, knowing it meant a more certain income for his family than freelance advertising art. In addition to his lack of ardor for the ape man, Foster had a low opinion of comics in general. "Even though it was a cheap medium, it was a way of giving entertainment to a large number of people. And after all, when I quit painting for posterity there was no great furor." Foster's relative indifference to *Tarzan* is one reason why he accomplished what he did with the Sunday page. Not taking the ape man or the continuities various hands prepared quite seriously, Foster achieved a looseness and a relaxed quality which his later work has lacked. His idols had not been newspaper cartoonists, but illustrators like Howard Pyle and E. A. Abbey, men whose realism was always tinged with hero worship, whose ideal format was the mural. In his first *Tarzan* work, on the 1929 dailies, Foster had paid his respects to the likes of Pyle as well as to all the advertising art directors he's been working with. There is very little flow from panel to panel, most of the illustrations have a formal posed look, and Foster seems to be avoiding action. He most often selects the moment before or after action. There's a lot of sitting around. His Sunday *Tarzan* was different.

A page meant a full page then, so Foster had a good deal of space to work with. He took over in the middle of a story. Tarzan is fighting for his life against a horde of nasty apes. His old chum, D'arnot, happens to be flying over in a French navy amphibian. D'arnot leaps to the rescue, machine-gunning the apes Tarzan hasn't been able to slaughter. Something has happened to Foster in the two years he was away. The page is full of action, there are long shots, close-ups. Perhaps he decided to save his serious Howard Pyle mode for better things. Here in the *Tarzan* Sunday a major influence appears to be the movies. And like most good moviemakers, Foster gets interested in the props and sets as well as in the characters and the action. When early in 1933, he follows Tarzan into a lost civilization based on that of ancient Egypt, he has everything under control. The backgrounds are so impressive and the staging so expert that you can forget about them and enjoy the story and all its magnificent hokum.

Hal Foster's work was having an effect on the comic field, though, as Coulton Waugh pointed out, "the man was so good at his particular job that there remained little for subsequent workers to improve on, and very few have had the ability to come anywhere near him." Even so, many artists would try, most notably Alex Raymond. Foster attracted the attention of other syndicates as well. "The King Features general manager came up to see me one time. He wanted me to work for King Features. I said I had an idea but I hadn't polished it up yet. I was a little bit tired of Tarzan because I had no control over the hero. . . . So I was playing with the idea of getting my own story. . . . He said you don't really need a story at all, come with us and we'll provide a story. Well, that's just what I don't want. I want my own story. So he left and about two weeks later he called me long distance and said, do you have the story yet? No, I said, my gosh, you hardly got out of the door. A month went by, a telegram comes, 'Let's have the story.' I was being pushed, but then somebody was interested and I got to work on it. I did *Tarzan* ahead for a couple of months and in the meantime did six or eight pages of *Prince Valiant* and wrote the story for two or three months."

Foster quit Tarzan to join King Features and produce his own variation on the Arthurian cycle. "Comic strips like *Buck Rogers* and *Flash Gordon* were going into the future. I wanted to go in the other direction, backwards, to find someplace to hang a story that was sort of fantasy and fairy tale." Both Pyle and Abbey had illustrated versions of the King Arthur legend, so Foster was going backwards in his drawing, too, in a way. Like them he put the story several hundred years up from the supposed date of Arthur's alleged reign—since the costumes and pageantry are better in the later period. The early *Prince Valiant* pages—it began on February 13, 1937—had some of the spirit of Foster's *Tarzan*. There is already a

516 12-8-35

Tarzan

by EDGAR RICE BURROUGHS

UNITED FEATURE SYNDICATE, Inc.

TIGHTENING BONDS

AS TARZAN WAS ABOUT TO TELL SIGREDA HE HAD RESCUED HER FOR THORIK'S SAKE, NOT BECAUSE HE LOVED HER......

......A THALGAARD FRONTIER PATROL ESPIED THEM AND RAN TOWARD THEM, CRYING: "HAIL SIGREDA OUR QUEEN!"

TARZAN KNEW THEN THAT THE KING, HER FATHER, HAD DIED OF WOUNDS SUFFERED IN THE BATTLE AGAINST ERIK THE RED.

BRAVELY SIGREDA SUP-PRESSED HER SOBS, FOR TEARS WERE ILL BECOMING TO THE RULER OF A HARDY VIKING PEOPLE.

NEAR THE TOWN, SHE SEIZED A WARRIOR'S SWORD AND TOUCHED IT TO THE APE-MAN'S SHOULDER, SAYING: "HENCEFORTH, THOU ART PRINCE TARZAN!"

AND TO THE PEOPLE SHE SAID: "WE SHALL BE WED, AND HE SHALL RULE BY MY SIDE, SHARING MY WEALTH AND SOVEREIGNTY."

THEN A GREATER CHEER WENT UP FROM THE VIKING HORDE: "HAIL PRINCE TARZAN! HAIL THE BRIDE AND BRIDEGROOM!"

AND IN THE THRONG WAS THORIK, WHO RUSHED ANGRILY TOWARD TARZAN, SHOUTING FOR ALL TO HEAR:

"YOU VOWED TO WATCH OVER HER FOR MY SAKE; AND NOW YOU HAVE STOLEN HER LOVE--TO GAIN POWER AND RICHES."

TARZAN WAS PERPLEXED. TO SAY NOW THAT HE HAD NOT SOUGHT HER HAND WOULD BRING SHAME TO THE ADMIRABLE SIGREDA.

HE GLANCED HASTILY ABOUT HIM, PLANNING TO FLEE FOREVER FROM THIS LAND OF FIERY HEARTS

BUT THORIK FIXED HIM WITH A COLD STARE AND SAID: "THE BLOT ON SIGREDA'S HONOR CAN BE CLEANSED ONLY BY YOUR BLOOD!"

NEXT WEEK: A CRUEL DILEMMA

Hal Foster seems to be warming up for Prince Valiant *in this late 1935* Tarzan *Sunday. © 1935 Edgar Rice Burroughs, Inc. Reprinted by permission.*

SHE SAW HIS ARM WHIP AROUND THE LEOPARD'S THROTTLE THE STRUGGLING BEAST.

HE ASCENDED THEN TO THE ASTONISHED, TREMBLING GIRL WHO FOUND COMFORT IN HIS NEARNESS.

THE DAYS THAT FOLLOWED WERE FOR LINDA A JUNGLE IDYLL. SHE EXULTED IN THE FREEDOM OF THE PRIMITIVE WORLD.

DELIGHTED IN THE SOCIETY OF JUNGLE CREATURES WHICH HER COMPANION INTRODUCED HER.

UNAWARE THAT HE UNDERSTOOD, SHE OFTEN DECLARED HER LOVE FOR THE STALWART TREE-MAN.

TARZAN GAVE NO SIGN OF COMPREHENSION. HE HAD NO WISH TO EMBARRASS HER, NOR TO DISTURB HER EASY COMRADESHIP.

THEIR IDYLL ENDED ABRUPTLY. ONE DAY WHILE THEY FROLICKED IN A CRYSTAL POOL, TARZAN LOOKED UP---- THE POOL SURROUNDED BY A HORDE OF APES, WHOSE EVERY ACTION INDICATED HOSTILITY.

HOGARTH—

THEIR BLOODSHOT EYES FOCUSED ON LINDA, AND THEIR LIPS MUMBLED THE AWFUL "DUM-DUM!"—THE DANCE OF DEATH!

Muscles and foliage by the Michelangelo of the funnies. © 1939 Edgar Rice Burroughs, Inc. Reprinted by permission.

stiffness, though, a tendency to strike poses. Crowd scenes look like tableaus. Then there is Val himself, looking more like Tyrone Power in drag than a heroic figure. So much for *Prince Valiant*.

Yet another artist with an advertising background carried on the *Tarzan* Sunday. Burne Hogarth had studied with J. Allen St. John in Chicago, and he'd done a previous comic strip. It was *Pieces of Eight* by pirate expert Charles B. Driscoll, the drawing of which Hogarth had taken over from the marvelously named Montfort Amory. Much respected in Europe even today, Hogarth is a vainglorious man with a considerable delight in his own abilities. He once explained to

51

me why his drawing in *Tarzan* was better than Michelangelo's. It has something to do with the fact that Tarzan's feet never touch the ground. Hogarth imitated Foster for a few months before unleashing his own style. A rococo thing full of twisting, swirling lines, it gave a whole new look to *Tarzan*. A muscle fan, Hogarth spent as much time on Tarzan's pectoral structure as Foster had given to drawing an Egyptian landscape. He was also big on shoulders. Everybody is broad-shouldered in Hogarth's jungle world, even schoolgirls. The muscle obsession got worse as the forties came on. Hogarth's figures started looking as though he'd skinned off a few layers to get a better view of the musculature. He quit the page in the middle 1940s, and was replaced by the barely adequate Ruben Moreira, who wisely hid behind the pen name Rubimor. Hogarth, after trying an unsuccessful page about a muscular South American lad named Drago, returned to the ape man. His enthusiasm had waned, and he got several of his students at the New York School of Visual Arts to pencil for him. He quit for good in 1950.

Meanwhile, all through the thirties and into the forties, Rex Maxon had been laboring away on the daily. For a short period in the middle thirties, after an unsuccessful attempt to get a raise, Maxon walked off the feature. (If *Fortune*'s estimates are accurate, the two *Tarzan* artists and their writers were all sharing $800 a week with the syndicate.) William Juhré, working in a style even blander than Maxon's, pinch-hit. Then Maxon was hired back. The copy, which eventually came to be lettered inside the panels along with the pictures, was provided by Donald Garden until the World War II years. From then Maxon wrote the strip himself. He hung up his loincloth in August 1947. Thereafter a parade of artists, all of them comic-book alumni, took a crack at the ape man dailies. Dan Barry was the first (his earliest dailies were signed Hogarth, but Hogarth had nothing to do with them), followed by such as Paul Reinman, Nick Cardy, Bob Lubbers, John Celardo, and finally Russ Manning. Since 1950, with the advent of Lubbers, the same artist had been responsible for the daily and Sunday *Tarzan*. This enabled Celardo, in his increasingly slipshod fifteen years with the feature, to just about kill both the weekday and weekend versions. Edgar Rice Burroughs, Inc., brought in Manning—he'd been doing the comic-book *Tarzan*—and he managed to keep the jungle lord alive. The salary connected with the job wasn't enough, however, causing Manning to give up the daily. Rather than hire a second artist, ERB,

ARZAN UNDER FIRE

By Edgar Rice Burroughs

The fatal moment had arrived. Yvonne stood with the knife poised above the boy who lay helpless on the sacrificial altar. Already Gulm had given the signal, but the girl remained motionless, paralyzed with horror. "Strike!" the high priest repeated grimly.

"I cannot—I cannot kill him. I will not!" Yvonne wailed in anguish. Gulm, the high priest, was seized with mad fury. He would not be defied! "Strike!" he thundered; "or you die!" Dick looked up at the girl. "Strike!" he urged; "there's no other way!"...

.Even if Tarzan were free, he could not possibly reach the spot in time to save Dick. But he was not free; he was the prisoner of twenty spear-armed savages. And they were unswerving in their determination to take him back to a cell in the garrison town.

"Come! March," the chief demanded. Tarzan shrugged, as if he were resigned to captivity, but his cunning mind was teeming with thoughts of escape. There was only one way—a hazardous way. Failure meant certain death. Nevertheless, he must take the risk.

A daily by William Juhré, least known of the Tarzan artists. Even two later newspaper strips, Draftie *and* The Orbits, *failed to make his name a household word. © 1938 Edgar Rice Burroughs, Inc. Reprinted by permission.*

Inc., began the practice, somewhat ominous to anyone who believes the adventure strip is still viable, of reprinting old strips.

The appearance of Hal Foster in the comic-strip field has been hailed in most of the few histories as the first shot of a revolution. His work is supposed to have helped convince "syndicates that the old formats no longer sufficed to hold the reader's attention and that suspense and action together constituted the wave of the future." As we've seen, though, comics had been moving toward action and suspense for several years before Foster ever drew a great ape. What the success of the Hal Foster *Tarzan* proved is that you wouldn't be penalized for being good. You didn't have to be good, as demonstrated by Rex Maxon, but it wouldn't hurt. And Foster was good, on *Tarzan* at least, in subtle ways. Subtle as compared with the self-conscious, overblown stuff which newspapers had tried to pass off as quality art in past decades. Foster was also important in that he inspired a few other artists to try to do something first-rate.

Tarzan made the jungle fashionable. Several other adventurers took to hanging out there in the thirties. Lee Falk's Phantom moved in among the foliage at the decade's end, after fighting crime in other ports of call. Owing much to the pulps and the serials, the Ghost Who Walks arrived in newspapers in 1936. *The Phantom* was Falk's second success; he'd sold *Mandrake* to King Features two years earlier. That idea he'd come up with while in college, and he got the contract while on a trip to New York with his father. The magician strip was drawn by a St. Louis friend, Phil Davis, though Falk says he drew the first sample week himself. *The Phantom* art was by Ray Moore. Both artists tried hard to imitate Alex Raymond's drybrush look. So successful was Davis that Falk says he once caught Raymond swiping a panel Davis had originally swiped from him. The Phantom's costume, one of the first such in comics, has changed colors over the years. In the comic books it was brown, in the Sunday pages purple, and in Europe red.

King Features had a virtual monopoly on jungle strips. Raymond's *Jungle Jim* was theirs, as was *Ted Towers—Animal Master*. This latter Sunday page was billed as being written by Frank "Bring 'Em Back Alive" Buck, who had already turned his animal-gathering exploits into profitable books and movies. A likeness of Buck, complete with pith helmet, graced the title panel. Joe King was the first officer, followed by Paul Frehm, Glenn Cravath, and Ed Stevenson. Seems like nobody could stick it out long in that particular jungle.

Tim Tyler's Luck was a jungle strip in these years. Tim and his pal Spud had been hanging around an airport when Lyman Young's strip started in 1928. Now they were in the Ivory Patrol, tussling with the same sort of untrustworthy white hunters and crafty witch doctors that so vexed Tarzan. Lyman Young was even less of a cartoonist than his brother Chic. He very early took on a ghost. In the early 1930s it was young Alex Raymond. Though not the artist he later became, Raymond was enormously superior to Young. When he quit there was no possibility of Lyman's carrying on alone. More ghosts. The best of them, who drew *Tim Tyler* from the middle thirties to the middle forties, was Nat Edson. When fans have written enthusiastically about Lyman Young's work, it is usually the Edson material they are talking about (the two Sunday pages reprinted in Martin Sheridan's *Comics and Their Creators*, for instance, are both by Edson). Nat Edson had a pleasant Raymond-inspired style; he'd worked out a basic pretty girl which was all his own. His sense of composition, like many of the Raymond-derived artists, was not strong, though.

Chapter 4
That Buck Rogers Stuff

By COINCIDENCE, *Buck Rogers* and *Tarzan* made their funny-paper debuts on the same day, January 7, 1929. Here were authentic fantasy and science fiction being adapted to a new medium— authentic in that both these heroes were born in the pulp magazines. The pulps were the principal source of non-British, non-high-class scientific romances up until the end of World War II. Both new strips grabbed a large following, with *Buck*'s impact being so strong that even today science fiction is sometimes referred to as "that Buck Rogers stuff." The *Tarzan* strip, as we've seen, was handsomely drawn by Hal Foster. *Buck Rogers*, on the other hand, resembled something scrawled on an outhouse wall. That didn't matter. *Buck* was an idea whose time had come. It inspired multitudes of small boys, among them future scientists and science fiction writers, and set syndicate editors to thinking. What the writers and the scientists eventually wrought is beyond our scope, but the wave of space-rovers and zap-gunners who flourished in the thirties we'll get to after a short jog with Buck Rogers himself.

"When I began my long sleep, man had just begun his real conquest of the air in a sudden series of transoceanic flights in airplanes driven by internal combustion motors. He had barely begun to speculate on the possibilities of harnessing sub-atomic forces. . . . The United States of America was the most powerful nation in the world. . . . I awoke to find the America I knew a total wreck." Thus spoke Anthony Rogers when he woke up in the pages of the August 1928 issue of *Amazing Stories* after a five-hundred-year nap. He repeated his Van Winkle act a few months later, this time in a new comic strip entitled *Buck Rogers*. John F. Dille, syndicator of the country's first real SF strip, had noticed Philip F. Nowlan's novelette in the Gernsback pulp and asked him to convert his story into a comic strip. Dille decided Nowlan's future-shocked hero needed, however, a snappier first name. He borrowed one from the popular screen cowboy Buck Jones. Rogers overslept in the strip, by the way. In the pulpwood version he came to in 2419, in the funnies he didn't awaken until 2430. Either way, he was in the twenty-fifth century for good. Buck Rogers' America, in those early years while Nowlan was still getting used to tomorrow, was a strange place. Stranger than usual. There were flying girl soldiers who toted rocket guns and wore jumping belts, there was television and even electro-hypnotic machines. Yet when Buck wants to look for the missing Wilma, his other new friends help him into the cockpit of a 1920s biplane. Perhaps the airplanes were due to artist Richard Calkins (who persisted in signing himself Lt. Dick Calkins, U.S. Air Corps Reserve), since he was the chief artist on the *Skyroads* strip as well. In addition to contemporary airplanes, *Buck Rogers* contained quite a lot of Roaring Twenties racism. The wrecked United States was now ruled by the Mongol Reds, the twenty-fifth-century version of the Yellow Peril, "cruel, greedy and unbelieveably ruthless." The underground organization Buck joins is fighting against them. Next to exterminating Caucasians, the Mongols' favorite sport was breeding with them ("She is a perfect specimen! The Emperor will reward us highly"). The resulting half-breeds were scorned by Buck's organization pals. The Mongols went in for vivisection, too.

The potency of the idea of looking at the future was such, in those months while America was heading inexorably for the Crash, which very nearly wrecked the country five hundred years ahead of Nowlan's predicted date, that *Buck Rogers* very quickly became a popular strip. This in spite of wretched dialogue and artwork that set the teeth on edge. "What, specifically, did Buck Rogers have to offer?" asked Ray Bradbury, the nation's oldest little boy, in his introduction to *The Collected Works of Buck Rogers*. "Well, to start out with mere trifles . . . rocket guns that shoot explosive bullets; people who flew through the air . . . disintegrators which destroyed, down to the meanest atom, anything they touched; radar-equipped robot armies; television-controlled rockets and rocket bombs. . . . In 1929 our thinking was so primitive we could scarcely imagine the years before a machine capable of footprinting moon dust would be invented. And even that prediction was snorted at, declared impossible by 99 per cent of the people. . . . I am inclined to believe it was not so much how the episodes were drawn but what was *happening* in them that made the strip such a success." Perhaps it's as simple as that. *Buck Rogers* made it easy for readers to dream impossible—so they seemed then—dreams.

Dick Calkins had originally intended to be a civil engineer. He might have been a good one. As a cartoonist, even after years of practice, he never rose beyond amateur status. Anything passable in the *Rogers* dailies and Sundays was the work of his assistants and ghosts. He usually hired them young, operating on the sound theory that you don't have to pay kids as much as you pay grownups. His first pair of boy helpers were Zack Mosley and Russell Keaton, who labored on both *Buck Rogers* and *Skyroads*. The Sunday *Rogers* page, initiated some months after the daily, featured Wilma Deering, Buck's girlfriend, and her teenage brother, Buddy. Like the daily it was narrated in the first person, in this case by Buddy. "I, Buddy Deering, had joined the Boy Air Scouts division while my sister Wilma and Buck Rogers were in Mongolia," begins the premier Sunday page. Beyond signing his name to the page each Sunday, Calkins had nothing to do with it. The drawing was by Russell Keaton. In the middle thirties Keaton—we'll talk about him in Chapter 6—became the artist on *Skyroads*, and the *Buck Rogers* Sunday was taken on by Rick Yager, another schoolboy apprentice.

Nowlan and Calkins discovered Mars in 1930. In the daily continuity the Martians appear in the sky over Earth in strange spherical craft. The dominant people on the red planet are the tiger men, a semi-Oriental appearing bunch who believe the white folks on their home planet are "an insignificant race." After a couple weeks of hovering, the Martian tiger men landed, "marched out of their great sphere, and for the first time beings from another planet set foot on Earth. Little did we realize the turmoil they were to cause. . . ." Meanwhile in the Sunday page, where a separate story was unfolding, Buddy was wafted up to Mars in another of the spheres. "Like a stabbing flame the space ship leaped for the sky and shot towards Mars—and in it I began my first interplanetary

If you think things are bad now, wait until the twenty-fifth century, when Brazil will be covered with ice. Not only that, but Latin Americans seem to be speaking with French accents. Rick Yager ghosted this 1938 Buck Rogers Sunday. © 1938 by John F. Dille. Reprinted by permission.

journey. Fifty days later we drifted down on Mars, over the country of the tiger men, and before my eyes unfolded a scene such as no Earth man had ever beheld—strange people and amazing cities. Curiously the foliage was RED and the water a queer GREEN!" How fresh all this must have sounded to the average newspaper reader of the 1930s. Phil Nowlan had several decades of pulp predecessors to draw on, and he'd barely gone beyond H. G. Wells and Edgar Rice Burroughs.

Right here on Earth Buck Rogers had an impressive side career as a merchandising property. The *Buck Rogers* radio show first went on the air in 1932, promising listeners futuristic adventures in a time when "Earthmen, no longer tied to the surface of their relatively tiny world by the bonds of gravity, shall seek their destiny in the CONQUEST OF AN ENTIRE UNIVERSE!" Several actors, including Matt Crowley and John Larkin, portrayed Buck during the show's run. Venerable Edgar Stehli was Buck's chuckling mentor, Dr. Huer. The Sunday pages were reprinted in comic books, including the forerunner of most reprint comic books, *Famous Funnies*, and the dailies were transformed into Big Little Books. There were Buck Rogers toys. A whole arsenal of assorted zap guns, plus watches, bikes, and wagons. Both the radio show and the strip offered a club, the Solar Scouts, for kids to join. Volunteers received "enlistment papers, including the SECRET SIGN, the SECRET PASSWORD, the SECRET SIGNAL and SPECIAL ORDER No. 1," as well as information on how to earn medals and such ranks as Chief Explorer, Space Ship Commander, and member of the Supreme Inner Circle. While boys could rise in the organization, the only rank open to girls was Interplanetary Nurse.

Phil Nowlan died in 1940; Dick Calkins quit the strip a few years later. Rick Yager, allowed to sign his work at long last, carried on. Murphy Anderson, surely one of the stodgiest and most unimaginative of SF artists, had a couple of cracks at drawing Buck. Then, in the spring of 1959, George Tuska came along to look after Buck Rogers during his final years. The writing passed from hand to hand, with science fiction writers, such as Fritz Leiber, doing sequences. The strip held on until 1967, living to see a good many of its gadgets and predictions become realities.

The Hearst organization, always quick to spot a trend, turned to science fiction strips in the early thirties. Their initial attempt at a *Buck Rogers*-type strip was tried out in the sticks first. *Brick*

Bradford was introduced in 1933 by the Central Press Association, Hearst's small-town syndicate. Although Brick did appear in a few of the larger Hearst newspapers, it was in the many lesser papers that he made his early impact. The hick syndicate was offering a *Frank Merriwell* strip at the same time, and there is something of that strong-jawed, clean-living leftover from an earlier era in the redheaded Brick. It took Brick quite a few years to get out into space; in his early adventures he was "a young American castaway in a lost world." He spent a good deal of time in the Land of the Lost, a place rich in monsters, wizards, pirates, and damsels in distress—the sort of location A. Merritt had been offering guided tours of in the pages of the Munsey pulps for the past decade and more. As the 1930s wore on, Brick Bradford visited other out-of-the-way places—the Middle of the Earth, the reign of Queen Anne, and the year 6937. The time-traveling he did after he gained access to a marvelous invention called the Time Top. Designed by Professor Horatio Southern, the Time Top was intended to help him "unravel the secrets of the past and probe the mysteries of the future." Southern and his mysterious machine originally had a strip of their own. Titled *The Time Top*, it started as a companion to the *Brick Bradford* Sunday page in 1935. I have the idea the bulky machine must have, at some point, fallen down from upstairs and landed in Brick's panels. At any rate, by the late 1930s he and Professor Southern and lovely April Southern were spinning their way through time and space.

The *Brick Bradford* adventures were drawn by Clarence Gray, in a pulpy drybrush style. A redhead like his hero, Gray had been a staff artist on the *Toledo News Bee*. William Ritt took care of the writing. He'd put in time on several newspapers and kept his job as editor and columnist on a Cleveland newspaper throughout most of the years he scripted *Brick Bradford*. A student of history and mythology, and a borrower from the works of Merritt and Burroughs, Ritt tried to be a little slangy in his dialogue, having everybody address each other as "kid" during one such spell. In his descriptive passages he let his flowery side show through: "The acceleration of the Time Top is so rapid that soon day and night blend into a gray-blue continuous twilight! The sun and moon are now but bands of gold across the sky. Time races on! Centuries are but hours! Generations of the outside world but a few minutes to those within the whirling top! Slowly a magnificent city rises on the nearby plain. It stands for a little while in ghostly beauty in the twilight of compressed time—and then vanishes into the dust from which it arose!" When Gray died in the early 1950s, Paul Norris picked up the art chores. As of this writing the strip is still appearing, although once again mostly in small-town newspapers.

A science fiction strip that matched *Buck Rogers* in awfulness of writing and drawing, though not in popularity, was *Jack Swift*. An early 1930s offering of the Ledger Syndicate, the strip's awful continuity was by Cliff Farrell and its awful art by Hal Colson. Jack, possibly a poor relation of Tom Swift, was a brilliant young inventor. His major invention was a rocket ship which was "a combined airship, stream-lined bus, vessel, and submarine." The first thing Jack and his comrades did once the ship was completed was to head for the Antarctic to substantiate Jack's theory that "the Antarctic was once part of the ancient land of Mu." A great many perils befell them, not the least of which was capture by giant penguins.

A much better looking SF feature, though no smarter in the script department, was *Flash Gordon*. It began, as a Sunday page, on January 7, 1934. "World Comes to End," announced a newspaper headline in the first panel. "Strange New Planet Rushing toward Earth— Only Miracle Can Save Us, Says Science." In movie fashion we are then shown shots of the African jungles "as howling blacks await their doom," the Arabian desert, where "the Arab . . . faces Mecca and prays for salvation," and Times Square, where "a seething mass of humanity watches a bulletin board describing the flight of the comet." All is not lost, however, since Dr. Hans Zarkov is working day and night to perfect "a device with which he hopes to save the world." As fate would have it, an eastbound airliner is struck by a meteor while passing over Zarkov's home. Among those parachuting from the ill-fated craft are "Flash Gordon, Yale graduate and world-renowned polo player, and Dale Arden, a passenger." What with one thing and another, Flash and Dale end up in Zarkov's backyard. Zarkov happens to have a rocket ship there, and he forces the pair to accompany him on a comet-busting mission. This results, eventually, in their landing on the planet Mongo. You wouldn't think people would fight over credit for this initial sequence, which is little more than a clumsy blending of Philip Wylie's *When Worlds Collide*, published in book form the year before, with a few assorted Edgar Rice Burroughs novels. Yet both Joe Connolly, King Features president in the thirties, and Alex Raymond later claimed they'd written it. According to Lee Falk, a long-time friend of Raymond's, Flash's adventures were written from the start by unheralded Don Moore.

Alexander Gillespie Raymond was in his early twenties when he drew his first *Flash Gordon* pages. Although he'd never signed a strip before, Raymond's work had been appearing in newspapers for the past couple of years. His last job before taking off for Mongo was ghosting Lyman Young's *Tim Tyler's Luck*, and that followed periods of assisting on *Blondie* and *Tillie the Toiler*. It was Russ Westover, creator of the latter strip, who got young Raymond a $20-a-week job in the King Features bullpen. The Raymonds and the Westovers had once been neighbors in New Rochelle, N.Y., and when Raymond made up his mind to try for an art career he looked up the older cartoonist. Before sending him on to King, Westover employed the young man as an assistant. What he paid him was probably even less than $20. Known as a cautious man in financial matters, Westover at least once had an assistant who worked for no salary at all. He had been able to persuade the youth that the experience of working with a real pro was worth more than money. How early Alex Raymond wanted to be an artist is difficult to determine from biographical accounts. He seems to have varied his life story with each interview. "I had no idea that I would ever be an artist," Raymond told one questioner. "When I was eighteen years old I went to work in a Wall Street brokerage office, and was a sad onlooker at the crash of 1929. After losing my job there, I tried to solicit renewals for mortgages, but this business was so bad that I soon quit and went to work for Russ Westover." Raymond told another interviewer he'd wanted to be an artist from childhood on. "I should say my father's encouragement was the greatest factor in making art my career. As a matter of fact, he had one wall of his office in the Woolworth Building covered with my drawings." In this version his father's death causes Raymond to abandon his drawing ambitions and enter Wall Street as an order clerk. However long Raymond had been drawing, his early *Flash Gordon* pages were not much to look at. The drawing was stiff, his inking uncertain, and correct perspective often eluded him. After a year or so his compositions grew much better, and he mastered the drybrush technique of rendering, an approach then much in favor among pulp illustrators and some slick men.

The appearance of *Flash Gordon* improved greatly. Not only was Alex Raymond drawing better, he was swiping from better artists.

Among his favorites now were Matt Clark and John LaGatta. From Clark's slick illustrations he borrowed a good deal, including the prototype for the new improved version of his other hero, Jungle Jim. LaGatta he used for pretty girls. Another reason for the great leap forward in the drawing of *Flash* was the hiring of the late Austin Briggs as an assistant. Briggs had been working, in such magazines as *Blue Book*, with a heroic style similar to the one Raymond adopted in the middle thirties. When I interviewed Briggs a few years ago, he was unclear about when he'd gone to work with Raymond and exactly how he got the job. "I think I met him at a cocktail party," he told me. And Briggs thought he'd been associated with the *Flash* page as early as late 1934 or early 1935. If this is so, a good many of the advances made from that point on are due as much to him as to Raymond.

While the pictures grew better and better, and the half-page stretched to almost a full page, the stories went right on being clunky. Although Mongo, with its castles and fluttering banners and deep forests, had a Ruritanian feel, the concerns of the 1930s also cropped up. Wars, invasions, dictators. Ming, the merciless emperor of much of the planet, was yet another embodiment of the Yellow Peril. His anti-white bias and his purple pronouncements made him a sort of galactic Fu Manchu. Don Moore's copy was plummy stuff and his dialogue ideally suited to the far planets, since nobody on Earth ever talked this way:

> MING: I see, Barin, that you've defied my orders that no man may let his hair grow!
> BARIN: Just because you're bald, is no good reason why we Arborians should go hairless!

> AURA: Father, why this sudden desire to see my son? Certainly, your interest is not sentimental!
> MING: Sentiment? Bah! I intend to take your son away from all parental care and place him under the supervision of my generals, so that, some day, he may succeed me on the throne of Mongo!
> AURA: No . . . no! Never! Ugh! You're positively inhuman!

It's probable that most of Flash's followers didn't pay much attention to what was lettered, in meticulous architectural fashion by Raymond's uncle, under the pictures. It was the pictures themselves—vast tableaus of lovely women and heroic men in fantasy palaces, scenes of lush monster-ridden jungles, and all that larger-than-life bravura action, all those adolescent dreams of romance and adventure so patiently given life—which seduced the readers. While not as widely publicized as Milton Caniff, Chester Gould, and some of the other top-grossing comic-strip artists, Raymond was one of the most influential. Himself an admirer of Hal Foster, Raymond inspired another whole generation of comic-book and comic-strip men. Raymond had made some attempts to move up into magazine illustration, but little came of it. He resigned himself to being a comic-strip artist and said, in characteristic fashion, "I decided honestly that comic-art work is an art form in itself, it reflects the life and times more accurately and actually is more artistic than magazine illustration."

Alex Raymond joined the Marines in 1944. One of his less gifted brothers carried on his *Jungle Jim*, and Austin Briggs assumed full responsibility for *Flash Gordon*. Briggs had already soloed on an occasional Sunday and had done all the artwork on the daily *Flash* strip, which got going in May of 1940. The writing on the everyday version matched the Sunday. The opening day shows Flash and Dale rocketing through the skies above Mongo. We cut inside the ship to hear Flash say, "Alone at last!" To which Dale replies, "I feel so safe with you, dear!" Briggs would occasionally initial his weekday work, but he never signed the Sunday page. "I was ashamed of it," he later admitted. Unlike Alex Raymond, Briggs couldn't drop his ambition to become a magazine illustrator. He stuck with Flash for four years on his own, then, when King offered him another contract, he turned it down. After leaving the syndicate he walked around Manhattan, feeling sick to his stomach and afraid he'd made the wrong decision. But he hadn't.

Mac Raboy, up from the comic books, followed Briggs on the Sunday page. When the daily was revived in 1951, Dan Barry, yet another comic-book alum, was given the drawing job. Don Moore kept on filling the Sunday page with his inimitable prose, finally being allowed a credit. Several people, among them Harry Harrison, wrote the daily adventures. On Raboy's death in 1967, Barry (and his large crew of ghosts) was put in charge of the whole thing. Like many who were bright young men in the 1930s, Flash Gordon is somewhat diminished today. It's likely that the Raymond-Briggs pages, reprinted in books, magazines, and newspapers around the world, have a much larger readership than the current *Flash Gordon* feature.

The *Brooklyn Eagle* (which was a newspaper, not a superhero) went into the science fiction line in the mid-1930s when it introduced *Don Dixon*. Though distributed by the Watkins Syndicate, the page had been cooked up in the *Eagle* offices. Several strips were created at the same time, supposedly because the paper was tired of paying other syndicates. John E. Watkins, formerly with the Ledger Syndicate, was brought in to handle distribution to other newspapers. None of the newcomers—*Gordon Fife, Bill & Davy, Tad of the Tanbark*—ever became a serious threat to King or United, and they'd all succumbed by the first year of the war. The *Dixon* Sunday was written by Bob Moore and drawn by Carl Pfeufer. It soon became an imitation *Flash Gordon*, although initially Pfeufer made little attempt to imitate Raymond's drybrush style, and for the first few months Don was an adolescent boy. Don then grew up, got himself a Zarkov in the person of Dr. Lugoff, and commenced having a series of mildly erotic sword-and-sorcery adventures. The decor was Early Ming, with lots of marble columns and towers. So was the costuming; the men dressed in Ruritanian outfits, most of the women like strippers. Bob Moore wrote about as well as Don Moore: "Blast you, you've had this COMING to you!" Don Dixon would exclaim when slugging a heavy: "Come on,

By 1941 Don Dixon was sounding pretty disgruntled.

you dogs!" "Come and get me!" a villain would taunt. All the continuities took place in the Hidden Empire, an amalgam of Mongo and Pellucidar. Don's steady girl was named Princess Wanda.

I've always been fond of Pfeufer's work, sloppy and hurried as it sometimes was. Considering the scripts he had to work with, he did a commendable job. He was also responsible for drawing *Tad of the Tanbark*, which, despite its circus title, was held mostly in the jungle, and *Gordon Fife*, about a gentleman adventurer. After the collapse of the Watkins outfit, Pfeufer went into comic books, where he drew such heroes as *The Sub-Mariner, Commando Yank, Mr. Scarlet, Hopalong Cassidy, Tom Mix,* and *Don Winslow*.

The least circulated science fantasy strip of the thirties was *Rod Rian of the Sky Police*. This short-lived Sunday page was done in the mid-thirties by Paul H. Jepsen as part of an eight-page ready-print tabloid comic section produced by the George Mathew Adams Service. The section, also featuring the work of Jack Warren and Al Carreño, ran in such papers as the *Metuchen* (N.J.) *Review and Raritan Township Sun*, which accounts for the fact that so few people ever saw any of its pages. The artist, after several weeks, changed the spelling of his last name to Jepson. His wife was interested in numerology at the time. Jepsen, who has long since returned to the original spelling, was in his twenties when he undertook the *Rod Rian* page. Recently married and living in Greenwich Village, he was working full-time for an outfit called United Theater Advertisers. UTA turned out mat-service movie ads, and among Jepsen's fellow workers were Stephen Longstreet and Carreño. Through Carreño, who'd come to New York from Mexico a few years earlier, Jepsen heard the Adams syndicate was looking for artists. He had a moderate interest in science fiction, so he suggested a *Flash Gordon* sort of page. Adams bought this idea, giving him $25 a week to write and draw it. This is the only newspaper strip Jepsen ever did. When it folded he went into illustration and commercial art.

Like *Flash Gordon* and *Tarzan, Rod Rian* avoided balloons. Jepsen was far from being a rival to Raymond or Foster, but he had a distinctive drybrush style. In the first page Rod is assigned to catch some space pirates who've "cost the Earth seven transport ships, many men and billions of earthons in Tellurium." The next week he is captured by beastlike aliens and taken to the strange planet of Mephistos. The first Sunday page, by the way, takes place in 2500 A.D. and the second in 2700. This time jump was apparently due to Jepsen's casual approach to the page rather than some sort of time

More trouble for Brazil, a deluge this time. Speed managed to survive the end of the world, but didn't make it in the funnies. © 1940 John F. Dille. Reprinted by permission.

LOOK! EUROPE IN THE DELUGE! THAT TREMENDOUS TIDE RUSHING DOWN OVER EUROPE FROM THE ARCTIC! THE PYRENEES ARE A RANGE OF FLAMING VOLCANOES!

LOOK! SOUTH AMERICA IS GETTING IT NOW! THE BASIN OF THE AMAZON IS A VAST INLAND SEA--- THE ANDES A MASS OF FLAME AND LAVA!

EARTH'S THIN CRUST COVERS MOLTEN MATERIAL THOUSANDS OF MILES DEEP. THE GRAVITY PULL OF THE BRONTON BODIES CRACKS THIS CRUST---CAUSING EARTH-QUAKES AND VOLCANOES!

THE WIND IS RISING NOW! LET'S LOOK OUTSIDE.

GO TO YOUR QUARTERS--- OUR OWN HOURS OF TRIAL HAVE COME! MEET WHAT LIES AHEAD WITH FORTITUDE --- WITH COURAGE!

MARVIN BRADLEY

26

machine. Fortunately for the sake of Rod's assignment, the Mephisians also turn out to be the space pirates he's after. Everything would no doubt have come to a happy conclusion if the tabloid section had survived.

In 1939 that runaway planet started heading straight for Earth again; a smashup looked inevitable. "The Earth will be shattered into fragments by the collision. . . . NO LIVING THING WILL SURVIVE." This time it wasn't somebody ripping off Philip Wylie, though. The John F. Dille syndicate, surely hoping for another *Buck Rogers*, turned Wylie's *When Worlds Collide*, written in collaboration with Edwin Balmer, into a daily and Sunday comic feature. The book must have seemed a likely property. Orson Welles had scared the more nervous segment of the population only the year before with his "Mercury Theatre" broadcast of *The War of the Worlds*, and this was even more unsettling than a Martian invasion. It's usually been true that a public worried about approaching large disasters will rush to be entertained by a fiction about an even larger disaster. Somehow, though, the strip never caught on.

Rather than name it after the book, Dille christened the feature *Speed Spaulding*. Speed, who doesn't appear in the novel or its sequel, is the hero of this saga of the waning days of the planet. Professor Bronson, the first man to become aware of the two spheres hurtling toward Earth (modestly dubbed Bronson Alpha and Bronson Beta), was transfered from the novel to the comic strip, not without having his name changed to Bronton. The writing on *Speed Spaulding* was credited to Balmer and Wylie, which is highly unlikely. The drawing, done in a creditable variation of the Caniff-Sickles style, was by Marvin Bradley. Not too lucky with Speed, Bradley fared better when he later teamed up to do *Rex Morgan, M.D.* No comic strip ever came to a more impressive conclusion than *Speed Spaulding*. Speed and his selected friends clamber aboard their spaceship hours before Alpha is due to strike Earth. They blast off, using atomic engines, and head out into space. In the final panel of the final strip the world blows up.

Chapter 5
Gangbusters

In 1931 Al Capone was tried for income tax evasion, Hollywood released *Little Caesar, Public Enemy, The Maltese Falcon* (the Ricardo Cortez version), as well as over fifty other gangster and detective movies, and Chester Gould, formerly of Pawnee, Oklahoma, sold a new comic strip. Gould, then thirty, had been trying to sell a feature idea to Captain Patterson for fully ten years. He finally succeeded with a crime-fighting strip he called *Plainclothes Tracy*. It was a hardboiled thing, full of gangsters, tough cops, tommy guns and fast cars, noise and violence—the same ingredients the movie studios, especially Warner Brothers, had been successfully peddling since the new decade of the thirties began. The hardboiled dicks were older than the talkies, though. They'd been flourishing, under such names as Race Williams, the Continental Op, and Sam Spade, since the middle 1920s in the pages of the pulp magazines, most notably in *Black Mask*. Like their successors in the talking pictures, most of the pulp detectives were a pragmatic bunch, impatient and plain-spoken. They talked not the language of polite society but of the streets and back alleys. Although Gould has never acknowledged the influence of the tough dicks of the pulps and the wiseguy hoods of the movies, his new hero, renamed Dick Tracy by the continually

71

tinkering Patterson, fits right into the tough-guy pattern of the early 1930s. In his very first newspaper appearance, on Sunday, October 4, 1931, Tracy talks in a tough, slangy style, takes a poke at a stick-up artist named Pinkie the Stabber, and solves a case for the chief of police.

Chester Gould had migrated to Chicago in 1921 to finish college. Although he majored in business administration, he went from school into drawing for newspapers. The years before he signed his contract with the Tribune-News syndicate, Gould recalls, were a decade of frustrating experiences in every Chicago newspaper art department except the old *Post*. "The first job was with the *Journal* where I filled in for a guy who was ill. He got well in 30 days. Followed a year in an advertising outfit; then, in rapid succession, I worked on the *Herald-Examiner*, the *Tribune* and the *American*. Stayed with the latter until 1929, when I moved to the *News*." While he shifted from paper to paper, Gould kept inventing comic strips. Some of them sold, some didn't. In 1924 he was doing a topical gag strip called *The Radio Lanes* for the *Chicago American*, and later in the twenties he drew *Fillum Fables*, which Hearst syndicated. Now he was getting somewhat closer to *Dick Tracy*.

"It was a burlesque on the movies," Gould has said of *Fillum Fables*. "I cannot claim originality for it. We already had a very capable man doing a strip like that—*Minute Movies* by Ed Wheelan." Gould's movie takeoff was one of several imitations—Segar's *Thimble Theater* was another—which the Hearst syndicates had initiated after Wheelan left. Gould's version, like Wheelan's, went in for continued stories which were parodies, mild ones in Gould's case, of current types of films—melodramas, Westerns, detective stories. Doing the strip meant Gould had to pay attention to *Minute Movies* and to what was going on in the movie houses. As early as 1927 he was using mock detective continuities. He didn't come up with a recurrent detective character, like Ed Wheelan's Inspector Keene, but he must certainly have been aware of what his chief rival in the newspapers was up to.

And of course there was also real life for inspiration. "Chicago in 1931 was being shot up by gangsters," Gould has recalled, "and I decided to invent a comic strip character who would always get the best of the assorted hoodlums and mobsters." What was needed, he felt, was a detective who "could hunt these fellows up and shoot 'em down." Amplifying on this, Gould has said, "We had a crime situation during Prohibition that was beyond coping with legally, or what you would call legally today. So I brought out this guy Tracy and had him go out and get his man at the point of a gun." He wanted "a symbol of law and order who could 'dish it out' to the underworld exactly as they dished it out—only better. An individual who could toss the hot iron right back at them along with a smack on the jaw thrown in for good measure." Besides being tough and impatient, though not much of a civil libertarian, Dick Tracy was unreachably honest. An honest cop was much needed in places like Chicago and New York, to name but two cities with less than spotless police departments at that time. Gould's new strip was soon a success in these markets, as well as in other urban areas. A few months after it began, the syndicate was telling potential customers that *Dick Tracy* had "caused more favorable comment than anything the *New York News* has ever used." They explained that Tracy was "the prototype of the present hero—but on the *positive* side. An antidote to maudlin sympathy with society's enemies, he creates no glamour for the underworld. Children love this character, and parents and teachers approve of him." Heroes who were impatient with red tape, particularly nice-guy vigilantes like Tracy, were extremely popular in the depression years. Gould's hero rose to success in the same years in which Clark Gable, Jimmy Cagney, and John Dillinger became national celebrities. By 1937 *Dick Tracy* was the syndicate's third most popular strip, topped only by *The Gumps* and *Orphan Annie*. In 1939, when Gould signed a new five-year contract, his strip had 160 papers, not to mention a substantial subsidiary income from comic-book reprints, toys, a radio show, and movie serials.

"Gunplay is a part of the strip, and was from the very beginning. That is natural," Gould once said. "The law is always armed. Back in 1931 no cartoon had ever shown a detective character fighting it out face to face with crooks via the hot lead route. This detail brought certain expressions of misgivings from the newspapers which were prospective customers. However, within two years this sentiment had faded to the point where six other strips of a similar pattern were on the market and the gunplay bogey had faded into thin air." While gunplay had something to do with the popularity of the *Tracy* strip, it was the increasingly violent and bizarre methods of dispatching crooks, and cops, which attracted readers, and news magazines. As the strip progressed through the thirties and into the forties, undercover officers were frozen alive in refrigerator trucks, smuggled aliens were sunk in the ocean with their own chains as anchors, rival crooks were doused with cleaning fluid and set afire, midget

DICK TRACY

By CHESTER GOULD

Fuel for Flames

A typical day in the life of Dick Tracy. © 1939 *The Chicago Tribune. Reprinted by permission.*

crooks were roasted in steam baths. There were also, of course, more conventional shootings (with the slugs going, as in Al Capp's *Fosdick*, through one side of the head and out the other), floggings, throttlings, bludgeonings, and an occasional amputation. Gould was also ingenious in coming up with ways to almost kill Tracy himself. Villains tried dynamite on the detective, decompression chambers, sulphur fumes (while Tracy is tied, spread-eagle, to an inverted kitchen table), exploding furnaces. They even dipped him in paraffin once. And there was Mrs. Pruneface, who chained the detective to the floor, then balanced a three-hundred-pound icebox on a spiked board resting on two large blocks of ice. "As the ice melts the weight of the refrigerator will press the steel point straight through his heart," the Widow Pruneface explains to her associate. "Oh, ha, ha!" he replies.

"I try to keep the detective deduction angle the main theme of underlying interest," Gould has explained. "Pursuit, deduction and action are the ingredients that I stress." Although Gould was a pioneer in the police-procedural detective strip ("I have a technician with the Chicago Police Department who spends one day a week with me. . . . We have continued to maintain a high standard of procedure in the strip"), it is his crooks and villains and not the authentic means used to track them down which helped put *Dick Tracy* at the top of the popularity polls from the middle 1930s on. After a few years of relatively conventional gangsters and hoodlums, such as Big Boy, Larceny Lu, Steve the Tramp, Stooge Viller, and Cut Famon, Chester Gould started fooling around with more flamboyant and exotic, also uglier, criminals—the Blank, the Mole, B.B. Eyes, Little Face Finny, Flattop, the Brow, Pruneface, and others. "People have asked me why I make my villains so ugly. My answer to that is that crime itself is ugly."

The success of *Dick Tracy*, not surprisingly, didn't go unnoticed. Other syndicates brought forth imitations. The closest and most successful imitation was turned out by another Chicagoan, a man of limited talent but considerable drive. Norman Marsh became a professional cartoonist after having been a career Marine, a prizefight promoter, and an agent for the Treasury Department. Speaking of some caricatures he did while in the service, Marsh said, "They weren't good, but they were enthusiastic." This also describes his work on *Dan Dunn*. Publishers Syndicate began offering Marsh's detective strip late in 1933 and by the spring of 1935 had sold it to 135 papers. While this didn't quite match Tracy's circulation, it meant

75

the strip was a substantial hit. Successful enough to annoy Chester Gould, who in interviews decades years later will still occasionally manage to throw in a dig at *Dan Dunn* ("It was an obvious copy of *Dick Tracy*. You've got to have a lot of guts to carry an idea through. And when you start imitating you lose your fortitude"). Marsh, however, liked to claim he actually invented the modern detective strip, in an independently produced one-shot comic book called *Detective Dan*. Since this black-and-white magazine seems to have been issued in 1933, Marsh's claim looks a little doubtful. He does, though, appear to have turned out the first original-material comic book in America.

Dan Dunn, possessed a profile which, except for a squarer chin, was almost identical to Tracy's. He looked as though he even patronized the same Chicago Loop barber shop. His hat was a little floppier, but this is probably because Marsh couldn't copy hats very well. Dunn's sidekick was a slight variation on Pat Patton, being dumber and fatter, closer to Fuller Phun in his cop roles. His name was Irwin Higgs. Dan Dunn, also known as Secret Operative 48, didn't limit himself to urban crimes. While he might track down a bank-robbing gang led by Ma Zinger ("With a fiendish light gleaming in her eyes, Ma Zinger levels her tommygun at Dan . . . "), he was equally at home battling villainous turbaned masterminds ("With a smashing left hand the great detective floors the cunning Oriental"). He matched wits with Spider Slick, "the brains of a monstrous gang"; Eviloff, a hooded arch-criminal who owned his own island, named, aptly enough, Eviloff Island; and the ultimate Oriental fiend, Wu Fang ("Wu Fang's a pretty slippery customer, Irwin"). I have the impression, by the way, that Wu Fang must have been a freelance sinister Oriental, working where he could. He showed up in silent-movie serials, detective novels, several comic strips, and his own pulp magazine.

The writing on *Dan Dunn* mixed the hardboiled and melodramatic styles. The drawing was godawful. Marsh never mastered perspective at all; the best he could do with a distant object was try to draw it smaller than a foreground object. Most often he gave up on backgrounds entirely, or, if in an ambitious mood, drew a little crack to indicate his characters were standing in front of a wall. Anatomy was another of his weak spots. Like most amateurs, he had terrible trouble trying to draw hands and feet. This is why there are so many waist-shots of people with their hands in their pockets in the early years of the strip. Full-face heads and three-quarter views were also beyond Marsh's abilities. So the profile shot became, out of necessity, one of his trademarks. If you glance very rapidly at *Dan Dunn*, it does, however, remind you somewhat of *Dick Tracy*. Newspaper editors must have felt this, since they bought the strip and kept on buying it for ten years.

With typical chutzpah, Norman Marsh also ran his own mail-order cartoon school in the thirties. One of his pupils was Ed Moore, whose career we'll look at in another chapter. In the middle thirties Moore got a job as one of Marsh's assistants. Jack Ryan, later to go to work for Chester Gould, was already assisting Marsh at the time, and the strip was looking a little better. The three of them turned out the feature, six dailies and a Sunday page, in a small room in a Chicago office building. Moore, who was paid $15 a week, says he had a very lively time during the months he was with Marsh. The first day he was there a former *Dan Dunn* assistant came by to collect some back pay. Before the money discussion was over Marsh had punched his ex-assistant in the nose. Marsh continued belligerent. When he heard the radio reports of the Japanese attack on Pearl Harbor, he made up his mind to go back in the service. "That afternoon I wired the Marine Corps in Washington, and three months later I was on my way to the South Pacific with a commission." *Dan Dunn* stayed home, drawn first by Paul Pinson and finally by Alfred Andriola. It gave way to *Kerry Drake*.

King Features, being King Features, could afford to try not one detective strip but a bunch. "I thought Brandon Walsh was off his rocker," cartoonist Will Gould recalls. "The syndicate wouldn't hold still for *two* detective strips! But Walsh convinced me that detective stuff was the hottest around." This was late in 1933; detectives and tough guys continued to flourish in the media and in real life. The Hearst syndicate, anxious to cash in on the trend, was willing to hold still for any number of tough detective and cop strips. The two Will Gould is referring to were *Secret Agent X-9* and *Red Barry*. Through Walsh, who was then writing the *Annie Rooney* strip for King, Gould found out that "Joe Connolly was looking for someone to draw a detective strip that was being written by Dashiell Hammett." Will Gould, an admirer of Hammett's books and the films being made from them, thought that was a great idea. "Well, I dunno," he quotes Walsh as telling him. "Joe Connolly's going crazy trying to get an artist to do it. They've tried out everybody, cartoonists and illustrators alike, including Russell Patterson and Jefferson Machamer. But Hearst won't buy." William Randolph Hearst, him-

Dan Dunn turned in his Tracy hat for a cap during the short spell when Alfred Andriola was associated with the feature. © 1943 Publishers Syndicate. Reprinted by permission.

self supposedly a fan of Hammett's, had instructed Connolly to get him someone to write something that could compete with *Dick Tracy*. King Features had already serialized some of Hammett's hardboiled fiction, and that had helped circulations. Hammett, who was devoting a good part of his time to drinking in this period, wasn't enthusiastic about doing a comic strip. The Hearst organization offered him a considerable salary and a free creative hand. Hammett agreed. Though he lived for nearly another thirty years, the continuity for the *X-9* strip was the last printed detective material he would ever write.

Urged by his friend Walsh, Will Gould decided to try out for the *X-9* job and showed a sample to Connolly. "Connolly liked it. I was given three weeks of continuity and told to go ahead . . . after first being warned that Hearst had the last word. I was paid for three weeks which were then hurried off to San Simeon." Gould knew several others were also submitting *X-9* samples. Among them was Alex Raymond, then in his early twenties and pulling down $20 a week in the King bullpen. While Gould was waiting to hear, Walsh convinced him King was willing to buy more than one detective strip and suggested he get busy on new samples. Walsh dragged him home, gave him several sheets of bristol board, told him to come up with something to show Connolly the next day. Knowing he had a reputation for being a procrastinator and, worse, a misser of deadlines, Will Gould sat down at his drawing board when Walsh left and vowed to work all night. "But some pals showed up just as I was starting to sketch. I didn't get back to my place till four the next morning . . . and I had to be at King Features at seven." Gould met Walsh up at the syndicate with a typed list of names and a drawing of two heads, side and front view of "a blond version of my *Secret Agent X-9* submission." Walsh was unhappy, but suddenly thought of a way to solve the problem. "He lit up one of his fumigating ropes and then started to trim the drawings with a pair of scissors. 'I'm gonna tell Connolly that you brought in a batch of stuff and then I cut these out so he wouldn't have to waste time lookin' at the others.' "

Several weeks went by, Will Gould heard nothing about either his *X-9* samples or the idea for a new detective strip, *Red Barry*. "One morning I get a call from Connolly asking me to drop in at a specified hour. When I got to his office, Alex Raymond and Dashiell Hammett were there. Connolly got quickly to the point: 'I'm gonna give you guys a chance to make some dough. Will, Alex is gonna draw *X-9*. You go ahead with *Red Barry*.' " Gould hasn't mentioned what his starting salary was, but according to contemporary accounts, Raymond kept getting $20 a week during the first months of *X-9*.

The *X-9* strip was finally ready to go in January of 1934. King Features announced it as "the greatest detective strip ever produced." Dashiell Hammett was described as "America's most popular, fastest selling author of detective novels." Alex Raymond got less space in the ads designed to sell the strip to newspaper editors, but the copy was equally excited about him pointing out that in his drawings "Hammett's story has been completely, masterfully realized."

By 1934 Hammett, who had written all the detective novels he was going to write, was garnering considerable slick-paper attention. A former Pinkerton detective, he had started writing for the pulpwood magazines in the early 1920s. He did most of his work for *Black Mask*, and it was in this pulp that *The Maltese Falcon*, *The Glass Key*, and his series about the Continental Op first appeared. Knopf began bringing out his pulp novels in book form in 1929. His last novel, *The Thin Man*, was featured in the slick *Redbook* in 1933. The hardcover version came out in January 1934. The photo of Hammett on the book jacket, with him looking a good deal like William Powell, was also used in the King Features promotions for *X-9*. Such then-prestigious literary figures as Alexander Woollcott and Sinclair Lewis raved about the *Thin Man* novel, and these raves were quoted in the *X-9* ads. The novel, featuring Nick and Nora Charles, also had the reputation of being dirty—primarily because Nora asks Nick if he got an erection when he struggled with one of the female characters. Knopf took out ads in the *New York Times* announcing that they were certain twenty thousand people hadn't bought the book in the past three weeks simply because of "the question on page 192." That sold more books. The publicity didn't hurt the new comic strip.

Hammett biographer William F. Nolan says, "Hammett combined the Op and Sam Spade in the character of X-9. H was cool, efficient, quick with a gun or a wisecrack and, like the Op, was a man without a name." Not only that, but during the first weeks of the feature it was even difficult to tell who X-9 was a secret agent for. Although he talks and acts like a pulp private eye when he is on a case, X-9 lives in a fashionable apartment and has a Filipino valet. When we first meet X-9 he is lounging in his apartment wearing a silk smoking jacket. The opening continuity involves him in protecting a millionaire. There are lurking hoods, an unfaithful young wife, a crooked lawyer, crooked servants, and a virginal blonde niece. Hammett was mixing bits and pieces of several of his pulp stories, tossing in a little of *The Thin Man*. The police don't seem to have any idea of exactly what kind of secret agent X-9 is either. After several weeks he phones someone called the Chief to report what he's into. The Chief, a plump, dapper man with a military mustache, appears in one panel. "That's funny," he is telling his equally dapper associate, "X-9 called up then stopped talking and rang off—Send a couple of the boys over there to see what's the matter." This is the last we hear of the chief, his dapper associate, or the boys. Eventually, after Hammett had quit the strip and G-men had become nationally popular, it was admitted that X-9 was with the FBI. By this time he'd given up the Filipino valet.

Hammett's working habits at that time may account for the sometimes cryptic and ad-lib quality of the continuity. Will Gould has described a visit he made to Hammett's hotel suite, at the suggestion of the syndicate, to get some advice on his own strip. "We did everything but talk comic strips," says Gould. "I kept mixing bacardi and ginger ales for friends who were continually dropping in. Producers, songwriters, artists, and—most of all—Lillian Hellman, who lived in the same hotel. . . . Hammett poured drinks and we went into a session that lasted far into the night. Mostly about fighters. . . . It was past midnight before we stopped. . . . He was beginning to slur his words, and his speech wandered. I helped put him to bed." By 1935 Hammett was no longer writing *X-9*. According to a contemporary magazine account, Hammett was fired by Connolly "when he lagged behind schedule with ideas that lacked the power of his printed work." Alex Raymond himself supposedly did the writing after Hammett's departure. He was followed by Leslie Charteris. By the time Charteris began writing, Raymond, too, was off *X-9* and concentrating on his *Flash Gordon* and *Jungle Jim* Sunday features.

The stiff and formal Raymond drybrush style had established a precedent for *X-9*. Indeed, as we've already seen, the King Features editors often wished everyone in their stable would draw that way. Naturally, then, they wanted somebody who could imitate Raymond to continue the strip. They picked Charles Flanders, who up to that time had favored a completely different style, and it took him years to get over the trauma of having to be another Alex Raymond. Then in his late twenties, Flanders had been in the King bullpen since 1932. He'd drawn a heroic, stylized *Robin Hood* Sunday page for King in 1935. It had a very brief career. In November of '35 he commenced on *X-9*. Flanders had an easier time emulating Raymond's inking technique than he did duplicating his compositions. His fairly well rendered figures huddled around in the middle of awkward settings, never quite fitting into the pictures. He hadn't quite mastered perspective yet either. But Flanders apparently satisfied Connolly and the rest; he remained on the strip for almost three years. We'll look at the remainder of his career, such as it was, in a later chapter.

Nicholas Afonsky, former Ed Wheelan sideman and also a protégé of Brandon Walsh, was already doing the *Little Annie Rooney* Sunday page for the syndicate. When Flanders was shunted on to other things, Afonsky added the *X-9* dailies to his work load. The figure of X-9 he swiped from his predecessors, all the other characters were done in his flowery version of the Wheelan style. Years of depicting put-upon orphans and wicked stepmothers had permanently affected Afonsky, and his *X-9* strips had a hammy, tearjerker look. Art Hokum would have been proud of him, but King wasn't. He kept the feature only a few months.

In November of 1938 Austin Briggs took on the strip. Briggs was at that point still working as Alex Raymond's assistant. When I talked to him in the late 1960s he no longer remembered when he'd started working with Raymond. He was certain, though, he'd been with him early enough to assist on *X-9* as well as *Flash*. If this is so, then the almost two years he now spent with *Secret Agent X-9* was his second stint on the feature. More restless than Raymond, Briggs, who was certainly the co-founder of the Raymond style, developed a much different approach on *X-9*. He moved away from the pulp look, closer to a more sophisticated slick-magazine approach. Rather than drybrush, he began using a lusher, wet inking. His compositions, which included down shots and tilted angle shots, were much more imaginative than anything that had showed up in the strip so far. Briggs worked on newspaper strips and pages for another ten years, but this was the only one he ever signed.

The writing of the strip had been credited for some time to Robert Storm. Tired of the shifting personnel on the strip, the editors had decided that one thing on the strip would remain constant. So they made up an author's name to stick on *Secret Agent X-9*. The writer who did most of the scripting under the Robert

Storm name was Max Trell, a former newsman and movie script-writer. He'd been writing, off and on, since the 1920s, and had even ghosted two autobiographies for little Shirley Temple. Detective stories were not his forte.

After Trell it was Mel Graff's turn to draw the strip. He took over with the release of May 13, 1940, in the middle of a sequence and after a week of strips by the King bullpen. Graff had been in New York with the AP syndicate since the early thirties. He was doing *The Adventures of Patsy* for AP when "Ward Greene, at King, both phoned and wired me" to carry on with *X-9*. Trell continued to do the scripts for a time. Graff told me he felt Trell "was doing a shoddy job on the story," and he eventually persuaded the syndicate to let him take over the writing himself. It was Graff who made X-9 somewhat more human. "You were supposed to love him because he wore a badge and carried a gun. He never fell in love," Graff explained in the mid-forties. "I'm changing all that. . . . Also, I've finally given the guy a name. After all, an agent who is supposed to be secret doesn't have everybody yelling 'X-9' at him. And so he will be known as Phil Corrigan from hence on." Graff had long been fond of this sort of name for a hero—Patsy's dashing uncle was named Phil Cardigan. X-9's love life improved as well, to the point where he finally married and fathered a child.

Under Mel Graff the strip swung even further away from the Raymond look. Graff, having worked with both Milton Caniff and Noel Sickles at AP, had developed his own individual version of their style. For a spell in the middle forties he also tried to sound like Caniff. His characters all began to talk like Hotshot Charlie on a bad day. When greeting an airplane pilot X-9 would inevitably say, "Hi, sky guy." A pretty girl would be called "a hunk of hubba heaven." Fortunately Graff got over this phase after a few years. Although Graff's most impressive work was on the *Patsy* strip, which we'll consider in a later chapter, his *X-9* was a consistently attractive feature. He favored, like his Florida neighbors Roy Crane and Leslie Turner, the use of doubletone board. Graff's staging of action was good, his design sense strong. He was also effective at depicting static stretches of continuity, such as office conversations, restaurant confrontations, and so forth. The strip, though, probably never did as well as Graff had hoped. By 1945, in a special drawing done for a Sigma Chi salute to Caniff, Graff described himself as "your stalemated old cellmate." Nevertheless, he stayed with *X-9* longer than anyone else so far. He finally left the strip in March of 1960, by which time he felt "the cops and robbers theme had grown tiresome."

Another artist who worked on *X-9*, though secretly, was Paul Norris, who backed up Graff. "In April 1943 I joined King Features to draw *Secret Agent X-9*," Norris told me. "I only drew the strip from April through August. From September '43 until January '46 I was in the Army." Norris went back to work for King when he left the service, filling in on a variety of features. "In the later part of '48 I started ghosting *X-9*. I produced the whole thing, story and art. I would do about two ten-week continuities a year . . . until Bob Lubbers took over the strip." Lubbers, a veteran comic-book artist and one of the fastest men in the business, was already drawing *Long Sam* for the United Feature Syndicate. He used the pen name Bob Lewis for his stint. In 1967 Al Williamson, who has devoted his life to drawing in the Alex Raymond manner, was given the strip. It became *Secret Agent Corrigan*, with Archie Goodwin as author. Williamson relies heavily on photos in his work. Since he is his own most available model, X-9 now has the same gawky build and slightly squinty look at the artist himself. If all the cartoonists who handled the strip had followed his practice, X-9 would have had an even more checkered career than he did.

Two months after the debut of *Secret Agent X-9*, King offered Will Gould's *Red Barry*, "a two-fisted hero in a detective-adventure strip that crackles with hair-trigger action, authentic atmosphere and thrilling plots." The promotion copy was equally enthusiastic about Gould. "For years, the famous sports cartoons of Will Gould were top reader favorites in papers everywhere. And now Gould's swift, vivid, athletic drawing and keen eye for human interest find their perfect expression in the smashing movement and exciting situations of RED BARRY's relentless war on the underworld." *Red Barry* was unlike any of the other detective strips of the period. It was a sprawling, freewheeling thing, not quite serious, a wiseguy strip. As time went on, and Gould got further and further behind his deadlines, the drawing became looser and splashier. "The first year I had been eager and ambitious. But from then on I created new records. . . . The cartoonist was required to be six weeks ahead, minimum. It was later stretched to nine. When I reached my 'peak' of about three, KFS wired that I would be charged for engravers' overtime." Gould, who migrated West after selling the strip, usually wrote his continuity late at night in one Hollywood restaurant or other. The *Red Barry* stories were a blend of tabloid crime, movie plotting, and pulp-magazine attitudes. Will Gould seems to have been influenced not only by Hammett but by Carroll John Daly, author of the Race Williams stories in *Black Mask* and *Dime Detective*. He even borrowed Daly's good-bad villainess, the Flame.

Gould was one of the first to letter key words in the balloons extra-heavy black: "Well SMART guy, get yourself offa THIS spot!" The habit later spread to comic books, where it still thrives. Red was described as an "ex-college football star, whose record as a gang-buster rivals his gridiron deeds." He worked in plainclothes, as an undercover man. His kid pal was known as Ouchy Mugouchy; the most frequent female character was a newspaper gal named Mississippi. The early stories tried to be as violent as anything in *Dick Tracy*, but, according to Will Gould, Hearst himself protested and the strip was toned down. Gould's continuing interest in golf and late hours got him into increasing trouble with the syndicate. He accumulated a large collection of urgent letters and telegrams: "Your daily schedule in bad shape . . . ," "How about your schedule? Please!" "You are two weeks behind." He hired an assistant, Walter Frehm, then ended up taking him along to the golf course and nightspots. Finally, in the late thirties, after a disagreement over subsidiary rights, Gould quit. By that time Red was not appearing in the strip at all. He'd gone away to recuperate. Ouchy and two of his contemporaries, known as the Terrific Three, had been solving modest crimes in Red's place. Gould drew a final Sunday page wherein the Three retire and split up. The last panel shows Ouchy asking, "I wonder when RED BARRY's coming back." King never ran the page.

In 1934, the same year they gave the world *X-9* and *Red Barry*, King Features took on *Radio Patrol*. The first adventure strip to star uniformed cops, *Radio Patrol* had begun up in Boston in 1933. Under the title *Pinkerton, Jr.* it had commenced in Hearst's *Boston Daily Record* in August of that year. The managing editor of the paper had come up with the basic idea. He assigned it to Eddie Sullivan, his night city editor, and Charlie Schmidt, who'd been in the *Record* art department since the First World War period. The editor gave the pair forty-eight hours to come up with the new strip. They did, turning in a feature built around the crime-fighting activities of young Pinky Pinkerton, his Irish setter named Irish, Sergeant Pat, and Stuttering Sam, partners in patrol car eleven, and Mollie O'Day, a plainclothes policewoman. According to King publicity, "two months after its initial appearance in the Boston *Record*, readers voted *Radio Patrol* winner in the paper's popularity contest over nine other strips with national reputations!" That sort of reader reaction impressed Joe Connolly enough to make him add the strip, under the new title he gave it, to the syndicate's list. Later on in its career the title was lengthened to *Sergeant Pat of the Radio Patrol.*

The *Radio Patrol* crew usually dealt with smaller crimes than their detective-strip contemporaries. Even so there was a good deal of action and excitement, and in the thirties the very idea of a radio car was much more enthralling than it is now. Writer Sullivan did have a fondness for involving his protagonists with a mad scientist now and then, but he more frequently had them going after pick-pockets, shoplifters, bank robbers, cat burglars, and hijackers. On one occasion car eleven even got a radio call to "go to Pier Thirty-One . . . thieves pilfering lobsters from fish loft." The red-headed Sergeant Pat shared the hero role with several of the other leading characters. Pinky, with his highly intelligent dog, frequently solved cases on his own. So did Sam, who in the best side-kick tradition was fat. Even more than the *Tracy* strip, *Radio Patrol* was filled with relatively accurate police procedures. Perhaps it was too realistic—it never managed to hit the national newspaper audience the way it hit those Boston readers in 1933.

The strip apparently didn't bring its creators a great deal of money. Sullivan was finally able to give his newspaper job up, but Charlie Schmidt stayed in the art department of the *Record* for the rest of his life. King Features publicity always mentioned Schmidt's workhorse nature. "His life in a nutshell has been thus: wake up, go to work in the offices of the Hearst papers in Boston, work all day, come home, eat dinner—and then start work on his action-packed adventure strip." For a strip drawn in his spare time, Schmidt's *Radio Patrol* wasn't bad. He had a moderately old-fashioned, non-spectacular style which fit the day-to-day sort of crimes Sergeant Pat dealt with. He imitated neither Raymond nor Caniff. Schmidt died in May of 1958, several years after the strip had ended. His last piece of published work was a two-page Easter spread of Jerusalem in the time of Christ. The patient Schmidt had spent ten years doing research for it.

The eagerness of King Features to add more detective strips and more famous mystery writers to their roster caused them to revive the dead in 1935. The result was *Inspector Wade* by Edgar Wallace. The prolific Wallace had died in 1932, but this did not keep the syndicate from attributing the new Scotland Yard feature to him. The *Inspector Wade* adventures were drawn by Lyman Anderson, written by Sheldon Stark. As Anderson recalls, King had contracted to convert several Wallace novels into comic-strip form. The inspector became the hero simply because he happened to be the lead character in the first book Stark was given to work on. The novel was *The India-Rubber Men*, published originally in 1929, and Stark's funny-paper version was a very free adaptation. Little of Inspector Wade's humor and flippancy, or even his astuteness, survived, and almost nothing of the English waterfront lowlife Wallace had detailed. It took Stark about ten weeks to use up a novel. Once finished he would doggedly set about translating the next one into boxes and balloons. Anderson, who later did some impressive illustrations for the *Saturday Evening Post* and *Cosmopolitan*, was still earning his living as a pulp illustrator. The artwork has a spare drybrush look, too bland to be very compelling. When Lyman Anderson graduated to the slicks, Neil O'Keeffe took over the strip for its downhill run. O'Keeffe had already put in several years illustrating the *Adventure* pulp. His work, blacker, livelier, and better composed, improved the appearance but not the circulation of *Inspector Wade*. The inspector succumbed in the early 1940s.

Another hardcover mystery character had preceded Inspector Wade onto the comic pages. This was the insidious Oriental villain, Dr. Fu Manchu, offered in comic strip form in the early thirties by the Bell Syndicate. The approach was sedate. Sax Rohmer's books were chopped into little blocks of copy which ran in type, as done in *Tarzan*, beneath the panels. "'Tonight they will try to kill me,' Smith said as we sank down on the cushions. He tapped the perfumed envelope. 'Fu Manchu knows that I alone recognize him as the most evil and formidable personality in the world today, and understand how the yellow hordes of the East plot to destroy Western civilization. Look out of the back window, Petrie . . .'" ran a typical caption. You'll notice that *Fu Manchu* was one of the few first-person comic strips. The artwork, which admirably suited Rohmer's prose, was by Leo O'Mealia. A veteran of two decades in the newspaper art business by that time, O'Mealia had a stiff, painstaking, pen-and-ink style. He spent the later thirties doing comic-book pages, and was a sports cartoonist at the time of his death.

Cops-and-robbers funnies continued to proliferate in the middle thirties. For readers who wanted to get closer to real life than

How I contrived to divert the sword, I do not know to this day; but its mighty sweep sheared a lock from Smith's head and laid bare the scalp. With the hilt in my quivering hands, I saw the blade shiver against the stone floor of the tank and break into pieces.

Still clutching to the hilt, I looked to the and across the room—to the curtained door Suddenly the curtains were swept apart and stood Dick, disheaveled and hatless, and beside her eyes blazing with a sort of splendid mad was Karaman eh!

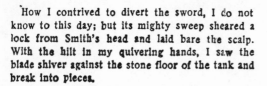

The Yellow Peril on the comic pages. Comparison of the last panel drawing with the copy beneath it indicates artist O'Mealia didn't waste much time reading Rohmer's prose. © 1932 by Sax Rohmer and the Bell Syndicate. Reprinted by permission.

either Chester Gould or Will Gould, no relation, could take them, there were true crime, and nearly true, strips. The Ledger Syndicate introduced *War on Crime*, written by Rex Collier, reporter and confidant of J. Edgar Hoover. The strip dramatized, somewhat in the manner of radio's *Gangbusters*, big cases which the FBI had worked on. While the continuities dealt with some of the more flamboyant and violent of the depression-era public enemies—Dillinger, Alvin Karpis, Ma Barker—much of the copy was bland.

Here's John Dillinger appearing posthumously in the funny papers. © *1936 Ledger Syndicate.*

A caption would state: "The FBI began a seemingly hopeless search. For their ultimate quarry was the Karpis-Barker hideout—supposed to be on such a lake. After dreary days on their strange quest, a squad of agents questioned a native of the town of Okla-wawa, Florida." The main fault of the drawing was that it was too good for this type of feature. For most of its run *War on Crime* was drawn, unsigned, by Kemp Starrett, certainly one of the most anonymous men ever to work in comics. Starrett had been a major magazine illustrator, as was his wife, before turning to newspaper work. In the thirties, working in a sketchy pen style somewhat similar to that of the Ledger's other favorite, Frank Godwin, Starrett ghosted several strips for this Philadelphia syndicate. After he left *War on Crime* it was carried on for a short time by Jimmy Thompson, another capable newspaper artist who, like Starrett, ended his days drawing for comic books.

A somewhat peppier strip, as you can tell from its title, was *The G-Man!* Written by a George Clark and drawn by Lou Hanlon, yet another veteran newspaper artist, the feature was initiated by the *Daily Mirror*, Hearst's New York tabloid. *The G-Man!* also dealt with kidnappers and bank robbers, with an occasional anarchist thrown in, but in a fictionalized way. The hero was Jimmie Crawford. As drawn by Hanlon he looked to be about nineteen (it's probable that author Clark was inspired by the *Operator 5* pulp magazine, which featured an equally youthful secret agent named Jimmy Christopher). The real G-men, broadening their operations in the 1930s, were now able to cross state lines in their investigations. Jimmie Crawford did them one better, working as far afield as Asia. Jimmie had a trouble-prone boy companion, like Dick Tracy's Junior. He was the G-man's little brother, and his name was also Junior. Jimmie's far-flung investigations brought him into contact with numerous women, such as Natacha the anarchist and Doris Kingsley, "richest girl in the world." His heart, however, belonged to a blonde named Mary. Their romance did not always go smoothly, which caused Jimmie to reflect that "a fellow in this game has no right to expect much! Mary is too good—too beautiful to be always waiting for a guy like me!" Hanlon worked in a semistraight cartoon style, and *The G-Man!* featured frequent action—speedboat chases, airplane dogfights, auto smashups. There was, though, a great deal of sitting around. The writing attempted to be up-to-date tough: "Scatter, you guys! The heat's on!" It was more often melodramatic: "Now to bring down the foreign traitor!"

Almost all the syndicates got into crime, even hole-in-the-wall operations. Lincoln Newspaper Features, Inc., offered *Detective Riley* by Richard Lee; the Matz Feature Syndicate vended *Be a Detective* by Bruce Patterson; and the Carlile Crutcher Syndicate had *Bela Lanan-Court Reporter*. Written by L. Allen Herne and drawn by Robert Wathen, this last strip was "founded on actual court records." It offered, in six-day sequences, real crimes. "You can be the judge," challenged the strip, the solutions being printed on a separate page of the newspaper each Saturday. None of the samples of this modestly circulated strip I've seen include Bela Lanan, so I have no notion who he or she might have been, whether a pretty young girl or a displaced Hungarian count. The middle-sized syndicates turned to detectives, too. McNaught acquired one who was already well-known in several other media.

In 1938 Alfred Andriola was twenty-six years old and working for Milton Caniff. Through a friend of Caniff's, he heard McNaught Syndicate was looking for an artist and a writer to do a strip based on the *Charlie Chan* character. Since Andriola wanted to be both an artist and a writer, he decided to submit samples. As Andriola recalls, at least a dozen other people tried out for the strip. None of them, however, had the advantage of having both Milton Caniff and Noel Sickles help them get their samples ready. Andriola was given the job. He heard about it while on vacation, Caniff sending him a telegram saying, "McNaught just bought Charlie Chan. That fixes you, but what happens to Pappy?"

Charlie Chan had been around since 1925, when Earl Derr Biggers sold *The House without a Key* as a serial to the *Saturday Evening Post*. All together Biggers turned out six *Chan* novels before he died in 1933. They are unexceptional, and had it not been for Warner Oland, Charlie Chan would probably never have become the valuable property he did. Oland, a Swedish actor who had specialized in sinister screen Orientals, such as Wu Fang and Fu Manchu, was the fourth actor to play Chan. None of the others had made much of an impression. Oland did his first *Chan* film in 1931. He proved to be, as William Everson points out, "a most engaging Chan. In fact, Oland provides the only real explanation for the continuing popularity of the series." Andriola based his comic-strip version of the Chinese detective on the Oland characterization. Though Warner Oland died the same year the first *Chan* strips appeared, the cartoonist continued to think of him as the definitive Charlie, making no changes during the five years the feature lasted.

While Andriola had read the *Charlie Chan* books, he didn't adapt any of them to comic-strip form. His Charlie was the movie Charlie. He also took the Number-One Son character from the Fox films, drawing him in the early strips to resemble Keye Luke. The rest of the characters were his own invention. Andriola soon found that "an elderly, philosophical Oriental detective was not ideal for a story strip. . . . A comic strip needs action." To this end he introduced, early in 1939, a second detective. This was Kirk Barrow, a prototype of Kerry Drake, "a vigorous, attractive American who can speak softly or forcefully, but still carry a big punch." From then on the daily strip co-starred Barrow. Son Lee, looking less and less like Keye Luke, appeared chiefly in the Sunday page thereafter. Unlike his mentor Caniff, Andriola had to keep two separate continuities going, one for weekdays and another for the Sunday page. Andriola soon learned you couldn't plot a daily strip like a mystery novel or a detective movie. In a newspaper feature, by the time Chan gathered all the suspects together for that final explanation of the case, ten or twelve weeks had gone by. Unless the reader were keeping a scrapbook he wasn't likely to remember who'd stepped through the French windows back in April. Therefore, Andriola kept the clues down to a minimum and emphasized action and simple suspense. With the Sunday page he was able to do a little more in the way of plotting. During the last years of the strip he took to telling Sunday stories that ran only two to four weeks. Often they weren't much more puzzling than the *Minute Mysteries* sort of thing, but these *Charlie Chan* Sundays come closer to being formal detective stories than most anything else done in the comics.

When the young Andriola began producing *Charlie Chan*, he'd had little actual drawing experience. "I started as a cleanup boy with Caniff," he told me. He'd done no real drawing while assisting on *Terry and the Pirates*. To help out with this new strip of his own he hired an assistant, Charles Raab. The ill-fated Raab had also worked with Caniff, and was a college friend and fraternity brother of his. A good deal of the work on the first year of the *Chan* strip seems to be Raab's. He did all the lettering, probably quite a bit of the drawing. Raab left in 1940 to do a strip for AP. The *Charlie Chan* artwork made a change at the same time; the next few years represent some of the best stuff Andriola ever signed his name to.

Whether this represents a sudden new plateau of ability for Andriola or a more gifted new assistant I'm not certain. Andriola assured me he employed no drawing assistants after Raab.

By the spring of 1942 Andriola was restless. He was tired of the epigrammatic old sleuth, wanted a character of his own. When he told McNaught he was going to quit they decided not to continue, even though Charlie was doing fairly well. *Charlie Chan* is one of the relatively few strips which was allowed to come to a graceful, rather than an abrupt, end. In the last panel of the last Sunday page Charlie and Lee turn to the audience, Charlie waves goodbye. The final caption says, "So Charlie finishes his story to Lee—the last story, for this is the end of the Chan series. And so, for the present at least, many thanks, and good-bye!"

Dick Moores used to be six feet three, though in recent years he's developed a stoop. He was born in Lincoln, Nebraska, "when bread was 5¢ a loaf," grew up in Omaha, and graduated from high school in Fort Wayne, Indiana. He worked with his father in the family wholesale radio business, managed a movie theater, and eventually saved enough money to go to Chicago and enroll in the Academy of Fine Arts. While in Chicago he became friends with a fellow cartoonist named Bob York. Moores, according to his recollections, was kicked out of art school, and when he next arrived in Chicago he was "broke and jobless." This was the early thirties; the depression had hit. York, who was now assisting on *Harold Teen*, told Moores Chester Gould needed someone to help out. "So I went to my basement room, shared with three other broke and jobless, and sat up all night lettering," Moores told me. "I took it in the next morning, and Chester hired me. Not because the lettering was any good, but because there was so much of it." Gould paid him $5 a week. Moores joined up just about at the start of *Dick Tracy*'s run. He stayed on for five years. "I did the lettering and backgrounds on the daily and Sunday and colored the Sunday prints. I never inked a figure." The characteristic *Tracy* style of lettering, carried on by subsequent assistants, seems to have been Moores's invention.

While working for Gould, Moores devoted his nights to working up samples of strips of his own, about thirty different ones. "None were accepted until I sent in one called *Jim Conley*," recalls Moores. The syndicates showed interest, and United Feature asked for further samples, next inviting Moores to New York. The name of the strip

This is the way most readers encountered Jim Hardy, *daily strips pasted up into pages for* Tip Top Comics. © *United Features Syndicate. Reprinted by permission.*

was changed to *Jim Hardy,* and Moores signed a ten-year contract. *Dick Tracy* was by this time, as we've seen, one of the most successful strips in the country. UFS felt a man who'd spent five years in close proximity to Chester Gould was just the man to do an adventure strip they could sell opposite *Dick Tracy.* So Moores did some sample weeks. At this stage Hardy was an ex-convict trying to make his way in the world. The syndicate ran off proofs of this version, the salesman went out. Nobody bought *Jim Hardy.*

"We changed him to 'a man against the world,'" explained Moores. In May of 1936 the syndicate ran ads in the trade publications offering this new improved *Jim Hardy.* "Announcing a new daily strip that is as true to life as it is dramatic! Within the last 21 months we have launched only one daily strip—'Li'l Abner.' It has captivated the nation. With equal confidence we now offer *Jim Hardy.* . . . Territory is closing fast." This time the United salesmen managed to sell Jim to three papers. "It was launched in June 1936, with a total billing of $27," says Moores. "We went into the red on it to about $4,000 by September 1936. . . . I started doing it for $25, I had been getting $75 a week. It never did get off the ground. It ran until October 1942, when I quit to go to work for Walt Disney. I was getting $50 a week by then."

The main problem with *Jim Hardy* was probably that Moores was somewhat too original. He was a much better artist than Norman Marsh, but he lacked the singlemindedness to do a one-for-one imitation of the successful Chester Gould property. This kind of flaw has kept a lot of people from getting rich. After drifting from job to job, Jim Hardy settled on the profession of newspaper reporter. As such he went after racketeers, corrupt politicians, and the like. Jim just couldn't seem, though, to act like Dick Tracy. He remained basically small-town, and Moores's small-town continuities didn't give the readers the kind of slambang stories that made them take *Dick Tracy* to their hearts. Moores would put Jim into a big-city story from time to time, but it was always a small-town boy's kind of big city: a wicked place abounding with shifty-eyed crooks, shyster lawyers, lurking white slavers, and wide-eyed virgins. Moores's drawing style, while similar in some ways to that of Chester Gould and some of the other cartoonists of the Chicago school, always had a pleasant folksy quality. He doesn't speak highly of his drawing in the thirties, but *Jim Hardy* was a nicely done strip, filled with many small touches which are Moores's alone.

The Jim Hardy character was never clearly established; even his appearance fluctuated. "As to the drawing of Jim, yes, I was a bit at sea," Moores admitted to me. "I couldn't decide how I wanted him to look—also I wasn't too good an artist." Eventually Jim wandered out of the strip entirely, relinquishing his place at the center of things to a cowboy character named Windy who'd been hanging around for a while. As caretaker of a racehorse called Paddles, Windy had to keep various villains from doing it dirt. In the final months of its life the strip's title was changed to *Windy & Paddles*—"mainly because we were struggling and the ship was about to sink." The ship sank anyway, and Moores got a job in Disney's comic-strip department. He did the *Uncle Remus* Sunday page and the *Scamp* daily at different times, managing to ghost for Virgil Partch on the side. In 1956 he started assisting Frank King on the daily *Gasoline Alley*, eventually doing all the writing and drawing. On King's death the daily became Moores's.

There were lady crime-busters in those days, too. None of them came right out and admitted she was a detective; they all fought criminals behind the façade of more acceptable professions. Usually they were reporters or nurses. In the middle thirties the NEA syndicate brought forth *Myra North, Special Nurse*. Myra's caseload was special indeed; she was forever running into master criminals, fiends, international spies. A simple house call would inevitably lead to her being assaulted by a crazed ape, an invisible man, or worse. Even some of her co-workers were not to be trusted. Dr. Duval, for instance, was conducting sinister experiments with Myra's sweetheart, Jack Lane, and the aforementioned ape. "Jack! It just occurred to me," Myra tells the man she loves. "I've read about scientists transferring monkey glands to men, but consider . . . what if this mad doctor somehow has discovered a way to reverse the process!" And what about Dr. Zero ("You know, Zero, if it wasn't for your colossal greed for gold, you'd be the world's greatest scientist!"), the man who has unlocked the secret of invisibility and intends to use it for evil purposes? Myra North didn't limit herself to hospital work or even private patients; she covered the world in search of new locations to be put upon in. She posed as a cigarette girl at the Purple Slipper and got mixed up in murder, hired out as a nanny to the most famous child actress in America, donned a Red Cross uniform in a nameless wartorn European country, was forced to be a lab technician in the underground Asian stronghold of the beautiful

Ming Sin, where "that ambitious lady herself is plotting one of the most amazing offenses the world has ever seen!" The writing on *Myra North*, a blend of girls' book and horror pulp, was credited to Ray Thompson. The drawing, which grew more and more hurried, was by Charles Coll. Myra gave up her practice prior to World War II, but Coll had one more fling with spooky detectives. He joined Street & Smith's comic-book staff, that elephant's graveyard of old-time newspaper cartoonists, where he was assigned to draw the *Shadow*.

The Front Page, and a flock of imitations on both stage and screen, promoted the idea that newspaper life was full of drama and excitement. Newsman detectives, as we saw in the case of *Jim Hardy*, didn't do anywhere near as well in strips as they did in movies. Girl reporters fared somewhat better. *Jane Arden* had a relatively long, if uninspiring, career. Written from its inception in the early thirties by Monte Barrett, former newspaperman and sometime mystery novelist, the strip had several different artists over the years. Frank Ellis, possessor of a flat, wispy style, was the first. Jane wasn't yet in the newspaper game when Ellis rendered her adventures, most of her intrigues being romantic ones. When a Sunday page was added, another cartoonist was put to drawing it. This was Jack McGuire, a much better man than Ellis. He did a capable job of depicting the Ruritanian escapades which then occupied Jane. By 1935 Russell Ross was drawing both the daily and Sunday *Jane Arden*. When I encountered Ross many years ago in Hollywood, I didn't think to ask him if he'd ever been a fan of Irene Dunne. His version of Jane, who became a reporter and crime-solver at about the time he assumed the feature, looks very much like a caricature of the actress. The Register and Tribune Syndicate, which distributed the strip, seemingly was never able to let anyone go. Ross had been doing an adventure strip called *Slim & Tubby* for them. When he switched to *Jane*, Jack McGuire went over to that strip. After the *Slim & Tubby* saga ended, the character Tubby got a job on the same paper with Jane Arden.

A more unconventional lady crime-fighter was *Invisible Scarlet O'Neil*. She began her career in June of 1940, a year after Clark Gable told Scarlett O'Hara he didn't give a damn. Owing something to both the movies and the burgeoning comic books, the strip was the creation of Russell Stamm. Stamm, born and raised in Chicago, went to work for Chester Gould while still in his teens. After some five years of that he sold his own strip to the Chicago Times Syndicate.

When he commenced the new feature his lettering was the same as that used on the Gould strip, and his backgrounds were nearly identical. It was as though he were using the *Dick Tracy* sets after the detective got through with them. Stamm's people, though, had more of an animated-cartoon, big-footed appearance. Scarlet herself, like the ideal screen woman of the early forties, had long hair and broad shoulders.

Invisible Scarlet, described in promotional copy as "America's new super-heroine," came by her phenomenal power because she was curious. "My father was a scientist," she explained in the first day's episode, "and one evening a few years ago I was in his laboratory when . . ." What she did was stick her finger in front of a "weird-looking ray." This particular weird-looking ray turned anybody who stuck their finger in front of it invisible, clothes and all. Fortunately for Scarlet she eventually discovered "a highly sensitive nerve in my left wrist." When she pressed it, she became visible again. The nerve acted as a two-way switch, so Scarlet could also use it to turn invisible. An invisible heroine might have been an opportunity to save on drawing for some, but not Stamm. He drew Scarlet even when she was not supposed to be seen, making her seem more transparent than invisible.

Stamm, like Dick Moores, displayed a sentimental side once he left the tough-guy climate of *Dick Tracy*. His early continuities involve helping kids with broken arms, saving blind boys from the machinations of their greedy guardians, and reuniting circus freaks with their long-lost mothers. The strip got somewhat tougher as it progressed. In 1944 Stamm went into the service. *Scarlet* continued with ghost artists. When he came back in 1946, his style was considerably altered—scratchier, less cartoony. The tone of the stories changed too, and by the early 1950s, when the strip was called just plain *Scarlet O'Neil*, it was making fun of the adventure and detective genres. In 1952 Stamm brought in a new character, an excessively virtuous Texan named Stainless Steel. Steel's mock heroics added twenty papers to Stamm's not enormous list, helping to boost his income to $40,000 a year. The strip title was changed to *Stainless Steel* at the end of 1954, and Stamm, at long last, got a little publicity, including a write-up in *Time*. He explained Stainless's growing popularity by saying, "His saving grace is that he isn't deadly serious like most heroes. He's got a sense of humor." Despite the publicity and the increased circulation, Stamm only managed

Scarlet O'Neil on the brink of becoming invisible. © *1941 Chicago Times, Inc. Reprinted by permission.*

to keep the strip going for little more than another year, and it ended in 1956. He gave up newspaper work and opened Russell Stamm Productions, where he created and produced television commercials.

The 1940s brought more detectives to the comic pages, both during and after the war. There were Kerry Drake, Brenda Starr, Rip Kirby, and Vic Flint, for example—different, most of them, from the hard-boiled dicks and the had-I-but-known nurses and sob sisters of the 1930s.

Chapter 6

"Been Around the World in a Plane, Settled Revolutions in Spain..."

THE ONLY TIME you hear about airplanes now is when one crashes or goes a few million dollars over its apportioned Pentagon budget. In 1927, though, all Charles A. Lindbergh had to do was fly one across the Atlantic and he made the front page of every newspaper in the world. Back then there was something called the romance of flying; people were enthusiastic about planes and aviation. It wasn't until the middle thirties, and not so much in this country even then, that airplanes in the sky weren't just something to look up at and get excited about. Flyers were celebrities in the twenties and thirties, like ballplayers, prizefighters, and movie actors. The astronauts, the daring airmen of our own time, are well-scrubbed, rather dull fellows. You have trouble, after the first half-dozen or so, telling them apart or remembering their names. But nobody ever mistook Col. Roscoe Turner for Wiley Post, or got Smilin' Jack confused with Tailspin Tommy. That romance-of-flying business was so strong in the years before and during the depression that people wanted to follow aviation not only in real life but in all the entertainment media. So there were air movies, air pulps, and a whole slew of air-minded comic strips.

"Lindbergh and some others were preparing to fly the Atlantic, and the Dole pineapple people were sponsoring a flight from the West Coast to Honolulu, so aviation was a red hot topic," recalled Glenn Chaffin recently. Chaffin, a former reporter and press agent, was living in Hollywood in 1927 when a newspaper syndicate rep got him together with a cartoonist named Hal Forrest. During the First World War Forrest had been a flyer, with the 144th Pursuit Squadron. After some barnstorming years as a stunt pilot he'd settled down to newspaper work and was drawing an aviation strip for one of the Los Angeles-area papers. The syndicate man had a hunch the country was ready for a serious adventure strip about flying. There was no major strip about pilots then, not very many adventure strips of any kind. Chaffin and Forrest agreed to try one. "We worked up a daily series—a dozen strips, I think, and the Bell Syndicate was enthusiastic enough to pay Forrest a small salary while we were developing the strip," Chaffin told me. "We worked sans title for several weeks when one night I was going over possibilities with Glenn Brownfield, a newspaper pal of mine. Out of the blue he suggested the word Tailspin. Almost at once I hung Tommy on it, as alliteration was the going thing in strips at the time." And that's how *Tailspin Tommy* was born. Starting in four papers in the spring of 1928, it "took off like a rocket and by the end of the year had fifty or sixty papers."

As to their working methods, Chaffin said, "I would write the script in dramalogue fashion. That is, block out the action, background, wearing apparel, etc. and write the dialogue balloons. I would take it over to Hal who lived just a few blocks from us in West L.A. and we'd go over it together. But it was understood that I was the writer and he the artist and mostly we were able to stick to that understanding." He and Forrest were equal partners. "We signed an original contract with Bell for a fifty percent cut of the take from the newspapers. It was a net cut for us, as cut and mat costs were taken out ahead of us. The syndicate later raised our cut to sixty percent, which Forrest and I split."

The main characters in the strip were Tommy, Skeeter, his flying sidekick, and Betty Lou Barnes, herself a capable aviator possessed of "more nerve than most men." The three were employed by the Three-Point Airlines, but were usually too involved with sky pirates, crazed inventors, lost races, and hidden treasures to put in much time with the airline's routine cargo-, mail-, and passenger-hauling activities. The strip got going when the talkies were catching on, which may account for the unusual amount of talk in the early continuities. There were dialogue balloons everywhere, bumping against the windsock, almost getting tangled in the propellers of the biplanes and trimotor jobs. The dialogue strived for up-to-dateness and a vernacular feel: "Jiggers! Here comes the princess!" and "It's a cinch! Those jazbos who knifed Don Q made a getaway!" The stories, though, were a mixture of sentimentality and thrills, which was as old, at least, as the dime novels of the last century.

"We had about 250 daily papers and around 200 Sunday papers when I sold out my interest to Forrest in 1933," Chaffin said. After they parted, Forrest continued *Tailspin Tommy* solo. His only gift, and a modest one at that, was for drawing airplanes. He couldn't draw people very well, he certainly couldn't write. Forrest's summary captions are especially nice examples of his prose. "Just as Tommy and Skeeter clambered into their plane a score of ferocious apes swarmed over the ship. Meanwhile let's return to Betty Lou, aboard the ancient hulk in the treacherous Sargasso. She is trying to escape from the clutches of the demented Old Man of the Sea . . . ," a Sunday page would begin. Another would commence, "As the bandit plane dove down upon Betty Lou's ship, pouring a hail of machine gun bullets into it, Tommy and Skeets, in their plane close behind and unarmed, realized that their pals would be killed unless a miracle happened." A Saint-Exupéry he wasn't.

Tommy had a modest career in other media, his newspaper exploits being reprinted in both comic books and the chunky Big Little Books. Universal filmed two *Tailspin Tommy* serials, in 1934 and 1935, with a clean-cut actor named Maurice Murphy as Tommy, and Noah Beery, Jr., as Skeeter. At the end of the decade a clean-cut actor named John Trent donned the helmet and goggles to portray Tommy in a series of four B-movies for Monogram. These films weren't very successful, and the strip itself was slipping by then. Forrest, still drawing and writing it, shifted from one syndicate to another for distribution. But he lost papers instead of gaining them. Even publicity pictures of him in a Tommy-type airplane helmet didn't generate interest. *Tailspin Tommy* faded out and disappeared from the comic pages about the time the United States entered the Second World War. Biplanes and barnstormers didn't mean as much anymore.

Another air pioneer was *Skyroads*, supposedly written by Lt. Lester J. Maitland and with artwork credited to Dick Calkins.

Some typical predicaments faced by Tailspin Tommy in the early 1930s.
© 1932, 1933, 1934 Bell Syndicate, Inc. Reprinted by permission.

Maitland, too, was an honest-to-goodness aviator. In June 1927, he and a fellow Army lieutenant had made the first flight from California to Hawaii, a twenty-four-hundred-mile nonstop hop in a Fokker trimotor. In the strip the lieutenant was given to addressing his readers directly, showing himself to be quite euphoric about the potentials and possibilities of flight. In introducing the feature he said, "Since the beginning man has struggled to conquer his environment. . . . Earthbound man has gazed fascinated at the limitless blue above him, yearning to ride the ocean of air. This generation has seen the age-old yearning realized. Millions upon millions of people now living will share the exaltation of air travel, either as passengers or pilots. And to all these comrades of the air I dedicate this work. 'God has given man wings.' "

The strip itself was considerably less oratorical, concerning itself initially with Ace Ames and Buster Evans, who "find themselves the owners of a new biplane" and form a business called Skyroads, Unlimited. "Some crate," says Ace of their new craft. Like the early *Tommy* continuities, these first *Skyroads* stories involved their heroes with smugglers, lost races of the Amazon, and similar pulp-wood props. Apparently Maitland felt the exaltation of air travel wasn't quite enough to grab and hold a newspaper audience, that the real-life flying adventures he'd had weren't the stuff of comic-strip stories. So he mixed in surefire cliff-hanger elements. *Skyroads* did, however, share some of the technicalities of actual flying with its readers: "When a plane is tail heavy, the horizontal stabilizers may be set at positive angle, raised slightly above the zero line or line of flight." The lieutenant also offered "my glossary defining words commonly used in avaition [*sic*]" and soon initiated a big flying club which would have "the largest membership of any aviation club in the country, and many famous flyers will be on its roster."

Unlike most strips, *Skyroads* never settled on one hero or team of heroes. It gave room to an assortment of daredevil pilots during its run of somewhat over a decade. In the late twenties there were Ace and Buster. By the early thirties, after Maitland's name had dropped from the credits, a youthful aviator called Hurricane Hawk took the lead (his name possibly inspired by the real-life Capt. Frank Hawks, nicknamed Meteor Man because of the many speed records he broke between 1927 and his plane-crash death in 1938). Typical of the villains young Hurricane tangled with were a gang of Asian bandits and their hooded leader, the Crimson Skull. The Skull was a crack pilot himself, and his orders to his minions to prepare his airship were a splendid blend of hanger talk and sinister Orientalisms: "Pull the chocks! Swing on the wing tip—I would turn in my tracks and be off! No bungling, you worse than nothingness!" At other times Hurricane concentrated on his flying, planning things like "a super stratosphere flight which might revolutionize aviation." Later on in the thirties Speed McCloud was the head man of *Skyroads*. Speed was a nifty pilot, though not always the most astute of men. He once fell in love with a female impersonator. In the feature's final years a new group of good guys took over, with a mature ace named Clipper Williams, a boy flyer named Tommy, and a skyful of others known as the Flyin' Legion.

Richard Calkins, who sometimes signed himself lieutenant, had joined the Army Air Service as World War I was ending. Out of the Army, he became a newspaper cartoonist and eventually went to work for the John F. Dille Syndicate. This Chicago-based outfit is the one that launched *Buck Rogers*. They made Calkins head artist on both that and *Skyroads*. A miserable artist, and overburdened with two separate strips to produce, Calkins wisely sought help. The two young men he hired, at very small salaries, were Russell Keaton and Zack Mosley. If you watch the early *Skyroads* strips closely, you'll notice Mosley and Keaton sneaking their names into the panels now and then, usually on the sides of boats and planes.

Several other aviation strips took off as the decade of the twenties came to its crashing finish and the bleak thirties began. The airplane was an obvious symbol of escape and opportunity elsewhere to the increasing number of people who were being both physically and emotionally immobilized by the depression. Among the new features were *Skylark, Flying to Fame,* and *Scorchy Smith.* The *Skylark* strip was by Elmer Woggon, who came down to earth in the thirties and, with considerable help from his friends, turned out *Big Chief Wahoo* and *Steve Roper.* Woggon told me, speaking of himself in the third person, "*Skylark* was the first aviation strip in U.S. papers . . . was not in illustrated technique but similar to *Skippy.* . . . He admits that *Skylark* may have survived longer in the illustrative style. Woggon's first sketches featured a blond little boy, but the syndicate insisted on adding six years to the lad's life. . . . Woggon admits that *Skylark* never really got off the ground. But he did try to show the science of aviation as to how planes act, etc." Various artists and writers worked on *Flying to Fame,* among them Russell Ross. It dealt with two aviator pals, called Slim and Tubby, who specialized in intrigues and little wars in the tropics and the banana republics. The pair had a variegated newspaper career. Under the new title *Slim & Tubby* the strip was a Western strip, a Foreign Legion strip, a prizefighting strip, and finally, after the advent of *Superman,* a superhero strip. Although *Scorchy Smith* got going in 1930, we'll look at it a little later on since its heyday was the middle thirties.

The best-known funny-paper flyer of the thirties and forties was Smilin' Jack, but when he first took to the air that wasn't even his name. And he required several more years after the name change to grow that mustache. He first showed up in 1933 in a Sunday page entitled *On the Wing.* The page was originally supposed to be a semi-humorous thing about three fellows learning to fly, though Zack Mosley began to swing toward adventure and continuity quite soon. When *On the Wing* was barely aloft Mosley got a telegram from Captain Patterson. According to Mosley the telegram said: "Change name of 'On the Wing' to 'Smilin' Jack!' " Mosley obliged, though he maintains he has no idea why Patterson suggested the new name. There was nobody in the strip named Jack, though one of the three novice pilots was named Mack. Mack was airborne, flying a rescue mission through a blizzard, when the transition came. The next week, still in the air, his name was Jack. And Jack it remained for the almost forty-year run of the feature.

Zack Mosley was born in Oklahoma the year before the state entered the union. He'd been enamored of airplanes since he was a small boy and got his first up-close look at a plane when one crashed outside of town, injuring the pilot. "In my mind aeroplanes were suddenly placed in the same category with rattlesnakes. I was afraid of both, but there was some strange fascination about them." Mosley's youth, whenever he wasn't handling the many chores that were a farmboy's lot, was spent drawing planes. He went to Chicago in 1926, using the $500 he'd earned after a year working in an Oklahoma City drugstore, and enrolled in the Academy of Fine Arts. He needed a job to meet his expenses while studying, was offered two: one as a "greeter and seater" in a restaurant, the other as a theater usher. "The decision was easy. I knew I couldn't eat those theatre cushions."

Next came the five years with Dick Calkins. "In early 1933 I visited my friend Chet Gould, another Oklahoman. . . . He said, 'You should create your own strip. You know a lot about aviation.' I agreed, but replied that I was afraid to fly. Chet said, 'That's great! Capt. Joe Patterson . . . is learning to fly. He's only cracked up a couple of planes.

107

I think he's afraid, too. . . . Start taking flying lessons yourself and draw a strip about scared pilots. The captain just might like it.' At the old Chicago Municipal Airport, I started taking flying lessons and froze at the controls only once. By midsummer I had finished a number of 'scared pilot' strips. . . . I drove to New York in a Model A Ford to show the feature to Capt. Patterson, and learned that he was going to enlarge the *News* from eight pages to sixteen. That was wonderful news. The only trouble was that over 400 other comics had been submitted. . . . The 'scared pilot' angle must have touched the late captain's heart, however. *On the Wing* was one of the eight strips selected."

Mosley had an extra edge, another friend plugging for him with Patterson. Walter Berndt, who was doing *Smitty* for the syndicate, had been acting as adviser to the captain, and he was helping select the new features to be added to the Sunday comic section. This is Berndt's version of why the Trib-News syndicate signed up Mosley: "Well, that's a wild story. There was one fellow who could draw airplanes very well. Zack wasn't so good yet, he was only a young guy but Zack had the ideas. He had action, adventure, the real stuff, etc., so I wanted to get Zack the job. Patterson liked the other guy better because of his beautiful drawings. So I figured out a little scheme with the help of my friend C. D. Batchelor. I told Batch that I planned to come into his office with Patterson with a drawing by the guy who did the beautiful airplanes and one by Zack. And that we'd ask Batchelor for his opinion as to which was best. I said, 'Be sure and pick the one on the right.' So Patterson and I walked into Batchelor's office a little later and I said, 'Batchelor, we need a little decision here—which one of these do you think is best?' As you can guess, he picked the one on the right, which was Zack's drawing."

After selling the new strip Mosley kept up his flying, getting his pilot's license in 1936. Whether or not his own experiences in the air provided him, as claimed by the syndicate, with ideas for the strip, they were certainly good for publicity. Mosley was continually being written up as "the flying cartoonist," and his picture, with him wearing the required helmet and goggles, appeared frequently in trade publications and client newspapers.

Mosley has often been accused of being a mediocre artist. This has led some to dismiss *Smilin' Jack* as being crudely done throughout its long career. An unfair criticism, since Mosley hired several quite competent cartoonists to ghost for him over the years. Most notable was Gordon "Boody" Rogers, who looks to have gone to work

There was always something going wrong in Smilin' Jack's life, in the air and on the ground. He couldn't even walk by a wind tunnel without getting in trouble. © 1938, 1939 by News Syndicate Co., Inc. Reprinted by permission.

on the feature when the daily strip was added in 1936 and stayed with it throughout the thirties. It wasn't the drawing, anyway, which made the strip a success. It was the bizarre characters Jack kept tangling with, the sexy girls, and all those airplanes continually flying around overhead. Mosley, no doubt influenced by Chester Gould, started introducing a weird lot of crooks and ne'er-do-wells in the late 1930s. Such scoundrels as the bald Lorre-eyed Head (it was as part of a disguise to catch him that Jack first grew the mustache), the one-armed Baron Bloodsoe, the sultry Teekeela, and so forth. Jack's friends and cronies were an odd bunch as well—the obese, button-popping Fat Stuff, the horny Downwind, whose face was never seen (Boody Rogers, by the way, had made use of a character whose head never fit into the panels, a variation on Downwind's cheek turning, in a strip he'd done a couple years before the debut of Downwind). Smilin' Jack's family was equally strange—his prospective mother-in-law once set a pack of dogs loose on him, and his brother-in-law left him to die in the Mexican wilds. Jack's romances, which often wiped the smile from his lips, were as ill-fated as those of any soap opera heroine. When Jack hopped into his plane to fly to his own wedding, you could be sure he'd (1) crash; (2) be set upon by sky pirates; (3) run out of gas; (4) be impressed into a chain gang; (5) end up a prisoner on Devil's Island; (6) all of the above. The girls he did manage to marry were usually lost at sea on the eve of the honeymoon. With all that romance, crime, and seat-of-the-pants flying, *Smilin' Jack* managed to outlast all the other aviation strips. When it ended, on April 1, 1973, Jack was a gray-haired old chap with a grown son who took care of most of the heroics.

Airplane strips continued to proliferate in the thirties. Hearst's King Features Syndicate introduced *Ace Drummond* early in 1935, a Sunday page drawn by magazine illustrator and World War I aviator Clayton Knight. It was allegedly written by Capt. Eddie Rickenbacker, WWI hero of the 94th Aero Squadron and killer of twenty-six German pilots, though he probably did little more than approve the continuities for this relatively dull feature. By late 1937 Knight was only doing the topper to the page, a true-life thing titled *Hall of Fame of the Air*, while an artist called King Cole took over the adventures of Ace Drummond. Cole had a cartoony style, and the closest he'd come to aircraft prior to this was when he drew Santa Claus's sled in the annual Christmas strip King Features offered. The Universal studios immortalized Ace on the screen in a serial starring

110

clean-cut John Kent, who had the habit of singing as he flew. The strip itself did not make it through the decade.

A more stimulating feature began in the same year, first as a local feature out in Denver and then as a King Feature strip. This was *Barney Baxter* by Frank Miller. An Iowan by birth, Miller shifted from job to job—bookkeeper, grocer, cattle rancher—and by the late 1920s was a staff cartoonist on Scripps-Howard's *Rocky Mountain News.* It was for the Denver paper that he started doing *Barney Baxter in the Air* late in 1935. The *News* had a Junior Aviator section each week and was running a series of model airplane contests. Apparently the new strip was originally intended to promote these activities. In this initial version Barney is much younger, an apple-cheeked freckle-faced kid of about twelve, and a Junior Aviator and model builder. After aiding a renowned aviator named Cyclone Smith, he is invited to accompany Cyclone on a flight to Alaska in his "trim little hydroplane." Getting his mom's permission, the ecstatic Barney takes off. Miller packs the strip with aviation jargon and enthusiasm matching that of Lieutenant Maitland: "With such marvelous inventions as radio and directional beams aiding a plane in flight—is it any wonder the world is air conscious?" All, of course, doesn't go well on that flight to the snow country. There are plane crashes, blizzards, and encounters with the first of a long line of bestial villains. This one is a half-crazed, ill-shaven aviator named Wolf Mongol. Barney survives it all. The first thing he does on reaching an outpost of civilization is call his mom long distance. "No worldly gift could bring such joy to Mrs. Baxter's heart as the voice of her son!" observes Miller. "And the happiness in knowing he is back safely from the adventurous flight is almost more than she can stand."

When Miller's Rocky Mountain editor was hired away by Hearst to come East and work for the *New York Mirror,* Miller was brought along. He began doing *Barney* for the paper, eventually for the King syndicate. Joining the *Mirror* aged Barney several years; he turned into an apple-cheeked, freckle-faced kid of about twenty. Like most of the 1930s funny-page flyers, he was something of a mercenary. If he wasn't involved in some South American air war, he was trying to outwit spies and saboteurs in his own country. Frank Miller was a patient and meticulous artist, in love with all the time-consuming pen techniques of an earlier era. His *Barney Baxter* is one of the great nitwit achievements of comics. He reminds you of someone building a Taj Mahal to stage a roller derby in, his beautifully rendered planes and action being used as a backdrop for some of the most godawful prose ever written. Besides Barney, who loved planes, his mom, and a girl named Patricia, there were two flying sidekicks, Hap Walters and a onetime desert rat named Gopher Gus.

America's entry into the war opened up new horizons for Miller. Instead of machine-gunning and bombing only Latins, Barney and his flying buddies could now also devote their attention to the Nazis and Japanese. They approached the destruction of their wartime enemies with a gleeful and childlike enthusiasm: "How did you like the way we annihilated those Nazi battleships, Gus?" "It was th' hot stuff, Barney! I couldn't not have done no better with my six-guns!" Miller, working several weeks ahead of publication, managed to second-guess Jimmy Doolittle and have Barney bombing Tokyo on the same day as the April 1942 raid. By this time Miller was living on a ranch he had bought in the Colorado Rockies. It was there in late 1942 that he suffered a heart attack and general nervous collapse. Bob Naylor, a King bullpen veteran who'd ghosted for Herriman, Harry Hershfield, and Ad Carter, took over the drawing and writing of the strip. Miller moved to Florida, where he eventually resumed work on *Barney*. He died at Daytona Beach on December 2, 1949, at the age of fifty-one. *Barney Baxter* was allowed to die with him.

Although Amelia Earhart flew the Atlantic alone in 1932 and Jacqueline Cochran won the Bendix Trophy in 1938, a girl didn't get to solo in her own comic strip until October of 1939. *Flyin' Jenny,* whose name apparently derived in equal parts from Mosley's hero and the Curtiss JN-4D training planes of World War I, was by Russell Keaton. A graduate of *Buck Rogers* and *Skyroads,* Keaton was a few hours of flying time away from his own pilot's license when *Jenny* commenced. Keaton—his nickname was Buster—had come up to Chicago from his hometown of Corinth, Mississippi, in the late 1920s to study art. While still in his teens he got the job with Calkins. "Keaton's childhood dreams had been similar to mine," Zack Mosley recalls. "We were finally drawing aeroplanes but we had never mustered the courage to ride in one, much less to become pilots. We began to feel like hypocrites. . . . One day after a local air show, a pilot was taking passengers up in one of the first huge Curtiss Condors. Keaton and I threw caution to the winds and got into the thing." This was Keaton's first flight. As an assistant to Calkins, as we saw earlier, he drew the *Buck Rogers* Sunday page and had a good deal to do with the *Skyroads* dailies. He took over the latter feature completely in the early thirties, and was allowed to sign it.

112

Jenny Dare got into the same sort of fixes as her male contemporaries, but usually wore fewer clothes. © 1942 Bell Syndicate. Reprinted by permission.

When he sold *Jenny* to the Bell Syndicate he was living again in Corinth. Initially he wrote the continuities himself, then Frank Wead came in to do scripts. Wead, a former Navy pilot and author of scripts for such movies as *Hell Divers* and *Blaze of Noon,* was later the subject of a John Wayne movie, *The Wings of Eagles*—one of the few comic-strip writers, incidently, to be so honored. During the war Glenn Chaffin did the writing. "Out of the blue Wead was recalled to the Navy to teach celestial navigation and had to give up *Jenny*," Chaffin told me. "I took it up almost in the middle of a sequence, but Wead had quite a bit of action mapped out." Chaffin, who'd been hired by Jack Wheeler, was living in Montana at the time. He and Keaton never met. "Keaton was wonderful to work for and with. We handled the whole thing by phone and correspondence." Jenny Dare, the blonde heroine, got into as many air races and intrigues as her male comic-page contemporaries, but she seemed to take off her clothes more often. Chaffin knew more about comic strips than he had in the early *Tailspin* days; his stories and dialogue were much better now.

Soon after *Flyin' Jenny* got going Marc Swayze joined Keaton as an assistant. Swayze was also a southerner, and he held a B.A. and master's degree in art. He left the assisting job in 1940 to go with Fawcett in New York. There he drew comic-book pages featuring various members of the Captain Marvel family, including the first adventures of Mary Marvel. During the war Keaton became a flying instructor, and Bell asked Swayze to do the *Jenny* Sunday page. Prior to this Gladys Parker, who'd drawn a panel called *Flapper Fanny* and was now producing the *Mopsy* panel, ghosted the daily and Sunday *Flyin' Jenny* for several weeks. Neither Chaffin nor Swayze has any idea why she was hired. Possibly Wheeler felt that if you can draw one girl feature you can draw any girl feature. Agreeing to take on the Sunday page, Swayze moved back home to Louisiana. "Some time later Russell called me saying he was going into the hospital briefly," Swayze says, "and wondering if I would take over the daily strip for a week or two. . . . Before the two weeks were up, his wife, Virginia, called and asked if I would continue the daily a while longer, since Russell would be in the hospital longer than expected. Her next call was to tell me he was dead, of a tremendously fast acting cancer." Keaton died on February 13, 1945. He was thirty-five.

Flyin' Jenny continued, with Chaffin and Swayze, into the postwar period. One of the final stories was concerned with Jenny's attempts to adjust to the civilian world. After cashing in her last war bond, Jenny makes the rounds of possible employers. She is told, "Sorry, Jenny, pilots are a dime a dozen." By the end of 1946 the strip had folded. "Somewhat mysteriously," feels Swayze, "as it seemed to be doing very well." According to Chaffin, however, the strip was finally discontinued because Bell and the Keaton family, who owned *Flyin' Jenny,* couldn't come to terms. "Too bad," Chaffin said, "it was a nice feature and one of the happiest writing experiences I've ever had."

The strip that was to have a major influence on adventure strips of every kind from the middle 1930s onward began inauspiciously and unhandsomely in 1930. *Scorchy Smith,* one of the initial batch of strips offered by the Associated Press syndicate, was the work of John Terry. Terry, the brother of animator Paul Terry and himself a former animator and political cartoonist, was one of the truly ungifted artists of the age. Scorchy, another of the lanky youthful heroes inspired by Lindbergh, attracted readers despite the clumsy and inept quality of Terry's work. By the end of 1933, when tuberculosis forced Terry to stop drawing, *Scorchy Smith* was AP's bestselling strip. Not wanting to tamper with it, feature editor Wilson Hicks looked around the art department for somebody to ghost the strip until Terry recuperated. He selected Noel Sickles, then in his middle twenties, who was doing political cartoons and general art for AP. At that time Sickles didn't know much about comic strips and didn't care, but he accepted the assignment. "I had to forget everything I'd ever learned about drawing," he told me, "absolutely everything." He didn't have a high opinion of his hero or of John Terry. "It was the worst drawing I had ever seen by anybody." Gritting his teeth, the young Sickles imitated his predecessor as best he could and signed John Terry to the strips. Actually it wasn't a very good job of ghosting. Sickles was so much better an artist that even his attempted impersonation was a vast improvement. When he took on the six dailies a week his salary remained what it had been in the bullpen, $42.50 a week. Terry died in 1934 and Sickles was allowed to sign his own name to the strip, but he was told not to change its look too swiftly. "Within that second six months on the strip," Sickles said, "I had to decide how I wanted to do it." His decision turned the newspaper-strip field upside down.

What Sickles began to develop in *Scorchy Smith* was the impressionistic, lushly black style which his friend Milton Caniff later appropriated for *Terry and the Pirates*. By the early forties the impact of the style was such that half the straight strips in the country were trying to imitate it. Coulton Waugh, in the AP fold at the same time, said, in discussing Sickles's work, "Impressionism is the substitution, in drawing and painting, of the appearance of things rather than work based only on knowledge of their structure. As an example, consider a steel girder on a railroad bridge. A worker in the old manner, knowing its rigid form, would rule out all the parallel lines, count up the rivets and draw them with careful, exact little circles. . . . In nature, however, light and atmosphere play tricks with forms, and the eye sees something that doesn't resemble a diagram at all. Sickles would see in the girder a pattern of sharp shadows; he would get the feel of those rivets by the little nick of black shadow which lies away from the light; suggesting this with an incisive touch of the brush, the whole rivet would leap with startling reality into life. . . . Of course it takes powerful knowledge to be able to do this well." In explaining to me what he was up to, Sickles said, "My reason for

SCORCHY SMITH

JUST POKING ALONG AT TWO HUNDRED AND TEN MILES AN HOUR, SCORCHY, MICKEY AND HIMMELSTOSS ARRIVE OVER FEZ, FRENCH MOROCCO ... SCORCHY SWINGS HIS SHIP AROUND AND LANDS ...

3-19   © 1936 The A. P., All Rights Reserved

—THIS HERE TOWN AIN'T MUCH DIFF'RENT THAN TANGIER —JIST A LITTLE DIRTIER, THAT'S ALL—

—ALL THESE NEAR-EASTERN CITIES ARE QUITE A LOT ALIKE, MICKEY — WE'LL GET SOMETHING TO EAT AT THE HOTEL AND TRY TO COOL OFF A LITTLE—

SCORCHY SMITH

WELL, MICKEY —IF YOU DON'T LIKE THIS HEAT— IF YOU WANT TO GO BACK —

NOW LISTEN, FELLERS— DON'T GIT ME WRONG! I WANNA SEE THESE HERE SHEIKS AN' TH' SCENERY OVER HERE —

3-20

—GUESS Y'GOTTA PAY SOMEHOW IF Y'SEE ANYTHIN' WORTHWHILE —Y'NEVER GIT SOMETHIN' FER NOTHIN'—THIS TIME I'M PAYIN' FER TH' SCENERY IN PERSPIRATION—

GOOD GIRL! C'MON, DOWN THAT TEA AN' WE'LL CLEAR OUT OF THIS RAT TRAP — WE'LL HOP OVER TO ALGIERS BEFORE SUNDOWN—

SCORCHY SMITH

—DER MEDITERRANEAN SEA, FRAULEIN! —YOU LIKE, YAH?

GEE, FELLERS, IT'S PURTY! —MAKES YA WANTA JIST LOOK AN' SOAK IT ALL IN —AN' NOT TALK ABOUT IT —

3-24   © 1936 The A. P. All Rights Reserved

Three days of Scorchy Smith *by Noel Sickles, exhibiting the style that had such an influence on his friend and associate Milton Caniff. The title of the third sample, with its allusion to "The Sweetheart of Sigma Chi"*

Wild Western Woman Versus Eerie Earringed Easterners

The Blue Of Her Eyes—The Gold Of Her Hair

song shows Caniff had an influence on Sickles as well. © 1936 AP. Reprinted by permission.

deciding on that style . . . was to make the strip more real. What I saw all around me were outline and solid blacks." And he wanted more reality than the traditional cartoon approach made possible. "I wanted to bring it out on the page." He also wanted to get emotion into the *Scorchy Smith* strips. He felt he was producing a romantic adventure strip, not merely a decorative one. "The thing that always triumphs is romance. . . . You have to go beyond drawing, beyond technique, you have to have feeling." There shows in all of Sickles's work of those years an excitement and a love of drawing. He was able to draw anything—New York street scenes, stretches of jungle, aerial warfare (he might devote an entire week of dailies to a beautifully staged dogfight), and, of course, people. "To be learned from Sickles, aside from his camera techniques, are the elements of body proportion, attitude and articulation," says Alex Toth, the most gifted of Sickles's disciples. "If I had to make a choice between anatomical accuracy and attitude, I'd take attitude. The body reflects thoughts and emotions—a mass of muscles doesn't." Sickles had, too, a very good sense of time and place. He could convey the intense light and heat of a desert noon, the shadows of a jungle afternoon, the feel of a big city in the early morning. He brought to *Scorchy* a sort of 1930s lyricism, a combined affection for the pastoral and the industrial.

Born in Ohio, Sickles says everybody in his family drew. His father painted, a brother was a machinist with a gift for mechanical drawing. "If you understand the construction of things," Sickles said in discussing his own interest in things mechanical, "there's no problem in drawing. But you have to understand the construction first. Once you have the basic shape, it's easy." Though he became one of the major magazine illustrators in America, Sickles's earliest ambition was to be a newspaper cartoonist. He spent as much of his free time as he could in libraries, looking at the work of every artist and painter he could get his hands on. He pored over everything from bound volumes of the German humor magazines to albums of the pen-and-ink sketches of Charles Dana Gibson. "I was influenced by all of them," he thinks, "not by any one." In his early teens he began to hitchhike to Columbus to visit Billy Ireland, veteran cartoonist on the *Dispatch*. Milton Caniff, a couple of years older than Sickles, was making similar pilgrimages, and it's in the *Dispatch* offices that they probably first met. Sickles, like a good many others we've covered so far, took the Landon cartoon course. This resulted in his working for six months as a mail-order instructor in the offices of the

Cleveland-based correspondence school. He next did political cartoons for local newspapers, eventually followed Caniff into the AP's New York offices in the early thirties. After Sickles took over *Scorchy Smith,* he and Caniff shared a studio together in the Tudor City apartments in the East Forties. Since Caniff was left-handed, the two cartoonists worked with their drawing boards facing each other and, as Sickles recalls, "talked all the time." They were both movie enthusiasts, often attended the all-night movie houses. "Sometimes we'd finish a day's work at midnight, go out on the town. We might wind up in Harlem or someplace. You'd get up after a few hours sleep and start all over again."

Sickles added several characters of his own to the *Scorchy Smith* cast, the most notable being Himmelstoss, a German ex-World War I pilot who was briefly a villain and then became Scorchy's sidekick. Sickles had been an admirer of Von Richthofen, and he saw Himmelstoss as a man who might have been a friend of the Red Baron. In some ways, Sickles feels, he was more successful with some of his second leads than he was with his star. "I could never make Scorchy Smith sound like a person. But Himmelstoss and some of those other characters I could make sound like people," he said to me. "Action was the most important, to keep the thing moving. More important than what was said, but the dialogue should read as people talk." Sickles did almost all the scripting himself, though Caniff occasionally lent a hand. The script was the easy part; Sickles could do that in a couple of hours. The drawing was what accounted for those midnight quitting times. It was not unusual for him to put twelve to fourteen hours of work into one daily. He didn't like to cut up a drawing or make corrections, so if a half-finished strip didn't satisfy him he'd throw it out and start all over again. He did keep Scorchy moving, involving him in adventures which ranged from revolutions in South America to treasure hunts in Alaska. At one point Himmelstoss and Scorchy both fall for the same girl, but it's the German who marries her. Although Sickles dealt with material similar to that of the other aviation strips, his story lines and dialogue were considerably more sophisticated.

By the middle of 1936 he was growing tired of *Scorchy,* and of the AP. He was still putting in twelve hours or more a day at the drawing board, though his salary had only risen to $125 per week. It was not the Associated Press' policy to tell any of its artists how many papers his feature had, nor were salaries based, as at the larger syndicates, on circulation. Sickles had been checking through all the out-of-town

SCORCHY SMITH   Counter Attack   By CHRISTMAN

newspapers that came through the AP offices, and he'd determined *Scorchy Smith* was running in nearly 250 papers. It was earning AP something like $2,500 a week. He'd been thinking lately of moving into magazine illustration. Since he had some money saved, he decided to quit. At the end of 1936 his name was no longer appearing on the strip.

His replacement also came from the AP bullpen. Allan B. Christman was about twenty, hailed from Fort Collins, Colorado. Everybody called him Bert, and he is remembered as being "a nice quiet kid." He and Sickles knew each other, though not well, and they never met again after Sickles left the syndicate. At first Christman's work on *Scorchy Smith* had a shaky, borrowed look. He soon, however, developed an effective style of his own, being especially good at

SCORCHY SMITH One Long Hop By CHRISTMAN

A pair of Bert Christman dailies. Scorchy got to China a few years before Christman. © 1939 AP. Reprinted by permission.

depicting the planes and other gadgets so essential to the strip. Restless, Christman stayed with *Scorchy* only a year and a half. Next he did a few jobs for the newly rising comic books. He was the first artist to do *The Sandman* in *Adventure Comics* and *The Three Aces* in *Action Comics*. This latter feature dealt with "three winged soldiers-of-fortune, sick of war and tragedy, who pledge themselves to a new kind of adventure. They came to roam the globe, working for peace and sanity." I've talked to both Gardner Fox, who wrote the scripts for those early features, and Vincent Sullivan, the editor who hired Christman. Neither of them could recall much about him, except

121

what had happened to him afterwards. Christman believed in a world where soldiers-of-fortune like Scorchy and the Three Aces could function. After a career in comic books even briefer than that in newspaper strips, he went to Pensacola for training as a Navy flying cadet. He then joined Chennault's American Volunteer Group, the Flying Tigers. Scorchy had done something like that too, back in 1937. He'd gone to the Orient to fly as a volunteer in the small air force of a Chinese general. "I interviewed General Claire Lee Chennault in Formosa for my post newspaper, while on leave, plane hopping to Hong Kong," Alex Toth recalls. "I asked him about Christman. . . . Chennault remembered Christman, a youngster insistent and eager for combat, but just not ready for it. And so he was kept in rear areas, training. Chennault yielded to Christman's urgings twice, resulting in Christman's loss of two P-40s, and it was back to training missions until the day he went up for his third and last combat mission." Christman's P-40 was shot down on that mission, which took place on January 23, 1942, over Rangoon. He bailed out, and a Japanese plane went after him and machine-gunned him. Christman, twenty-six now, was dead before he hit the ground.

It was a new world, no place for the grinning, slightly innocent air daredevils. There would be more flyers in the comic pages as the Second World War went on. But they were warriors, not soldiers-of-fortune. That had ended.

Chapter 7
Terry and the Pirates

TWENTY-SEVEN YEARS AFTER he stopped drawing *Terry and the Pirates,* Milton Caniff was still thinking about it. "In the middle 1940s, when I made the deal to do a new strip for Marshall Field, I had plenty of time to become used to the fact I would be giving up all the *Terry* characters. It was not unlike a parent knowing that his children were no longer legally his and that he must relinquish them by court order," he wrote in an obituary for the strip. "When I heard that *Terry* would be discontinued as of February 1973, I experienced the sensation of a parent learning his long-gone, but alive, children were sentenced to be executed." Caniff went on to talk about the people in the strip, characters who were as real to him as the children he might have had. "I sometimes think back on the plans I had noodled around with and wonder how they would have played out in print. . . . I planned to have Pat Ryan marry Burma. That would have been a *Taming of the Shrew* at jet speed. . . . There was never a Stateside story in my *Terry.* I was going to make a big thing of all these China hands returning to the U.S. and showing how the picaresque hero from the Far Places does not always fare so well in the conventional surroundings back home." Characteristically, Caniff, not wanting to sound too sentimental or artistic, concluded the obit by saying the real purpose of *Terry and the Pirates* had been "to force the customer to buy tomorrow's paper."

Caniff looked after the fortunes of the *Terry* characters from 1934 to 1946, not even half the time he's since devoted to his newer offspring, *Steve Canyon*. Yet they're obviously all alive to him, still important. Although he has continued to hold a fairly prominent position as an adventure artist and storyteller, that decade when the United States made the inevitable transition from depression to war was Caniff's brightest period. His talents and sensibilities were the kind to flourish in such a time, a time both cynical and sentimental, a time striving to be uninvolved and homespun while aggressive and streamlined. *Terry and the Pirates* was the best comic strip to come out of the adventurous decade. We'll get at the reasons why by way of the events leading up to its creation.

Milton Arthur Paul Caniff, an only child, was born in Hillsboro, Ohio, in 1907. In this small midwestern town, where he spent his first ten years, Caniff encountered several of the influences that shaped his life. His father worked in the print shop of the local newspaper. Caniff, who went to work in a newspaper art department at fourteen, thinks of himself as basically a newspaper man even now. The Hillsboro paper was owned by a man who'd been a Sigma Chi at college, and living in the town was General Benjamin Runkle, a Civil War veteran known in Sigma Chi annals as one of the seven founders of the fraternity. The Sigma Chi fraternity, which Caniff joined in college, is one of the most important elements in his life. His affiliation, as we'll see, helped him attract the attention of Captain Patterson of the *New York News*. Equally important were the trips his family made each year to California. They would spend their winters in Redlands, a Southern California town about seventy-five miles inland from Hollywood. One of the things the young Caniff did while living out West was extra work in some two-reel comedies. This introduced him to acting and to the movies.

When Caniff was eleven the family moved to Dayton, the city where the Wright brothers had had their bicycle shop. The Caniffs lived near McCook Field. The airfield had been designated an experimental laboratory the previous year. During the First World War and immediately after, several important aviation firsts took place at McCook, including the unofficial two-man altitude record and the earliest use of the backpack parachute. Decades later, in one of his special *Steve Canyon* Sunday pages, Caniff reminisced about that period of his life. "My earliest childhood heroes were of an ancient time; remote and fleshless symbols; strange in dress and tongue. Then, from the untracked sky came present glory—gallant as knighthood! Courage: raw and pioneer reckless. No saviors of a nation then, those crazy kids I knew when Dayton was the only place to test the birds." He devoted most of the rest of the page to a lyrical plea for not cutting defense budgets, ending with, "So much has happened since I sat upon the levee near McCook to watch the New Breed rise and break the natural law."

A few weeks after Caniff began doing the *Terry* strip, *Editor & Publisher* ran a very short biography of him. It said he'd "attended the Landon cartooning school and had his first cartoon published in the *Dayton Daily News*. When he was 14 years old, he worked as an office boy in the art department of the *Dayton Journal*. Mr. Caniff attended Ohio State University and later applied to Billy Ireland of the *Columbus Dispatch* for a job as a cartoonist. He worked for five years in the *Dispatch* art department while attending college. He joined a local stock company and then found he had to choose between art and the stage. . . . After graduation from college he did daily features and a Sunday theatrical feature for the *Dispatch*. He later went with the Associated Press, doing feature panels and cartoon strips, prior to joining the Tribune-News syndicate service." Although this gives some idea of what Caniff was doing in the years between sitting on the levee at McCook and going to work for Captain Patterson, it leaves out most of the important details. Caniff's enthusiasm for newspaper work was considerable. He'd been hanging around the *Journal* art department for quite a while, and then "at last I was invited to join the magic circle of insiders, instead of gazing longingly at the hallowed area marked Art Department!" While in college, where he majored in fine arts, he was art editor of the campus humor magazine, the *Sundial*, and also yearbook art editor. He also starred in several campus plays, and joined a touring stock company from time to time. "Strangely enough," he's said, "I became quite adept at this odd triple life—and learned quite a bit about entertainment. I had more irons in the fire than the village blacksmith." It was while talking over his love for the theater with the veteran cartoonist Ireland that Caniff was given the frequently quoted advice, "Stick to your inkpots, kid; actors don't eat regularly." Caniff did give up the theater, in that he stopped appearing on the stage, but he remained an actor and played all the parts in his strips.

Another young artist who came to Billy Ireland for mentoring was Noel Sickles. Caniff remembers him then as an unassuming, gangling country boy. "But, Jesus, could he draw," he told me. Caniff and Sickles were friends from then on. Sickles was even, until he gave up college, a pledge in the Sigma Chi house. "Sickles was never as gung ho about the fraternity." To Caniff, however, the vows he took on joining Sigma Chi were indeed for a lifetime. Both Pat Ryan and Steve Canyon are Sigs, and Caniff has built several plots around the Sigma Chi pin, which is shaped like a Maltese cross. "Big Stoop finds Pat Ryan's Sigma Chi badge," reported the fraternity magazine on one occasion. "Other national fraternities were in an uproar in summer 1937 when the Sigma Chi badge appeared in the Sunday newspapers in many college towns on the exact day most Greek-letter chapters did their pledging." A great many drawings, often featuring Pat, Terry, and even Big Stoop, were done especially for the national magazine of Sigma Chi. In one such Terry asks Pat what's so good about this particular fraternity. "I took a Sigma Chi pledge button," replies pipe-smoking Pat, "because of the alumni. . . . It's easy to be a hot fraternity man during the college period . . . but I figured a group had to *have* something to hold the interest of so many busy men long after graduation!" His feelings about his fraternity stayed with Caniff, joined later by a similar affection for the Air Force.

Caniff, who'd taken ROTC classes along with Curtis LeMay, was never eligible for military service. "I was bitten by a mosquito in the Everglades in Florida in 1925 and the bite became infected and I ended up with a double case of blood poisoning and phlebitis. It's been plaguing me all of my life and I find it a damn nuisance,

A 1934 Dickie Dare, *drawn before Caniff had come under the influence of Sickles. Dickie, before coming under the influence of his longtime mentor Dan Flynn, wasn't too good at picking heroes to pal around with.* © 1934 AP. Reprinted by permission.

but it keeps me honest." Though he couldn't serve, Caniff was to become one of the country's most active bystanders. "Although Milton Caniff is 4-F in the draft," said *Esquire* in 1944, "he is making an incalculable contribution to the war effort through his cartoon strip."

In the 1920s Caniff "batted around Europe, but I have never been to any of the places I have tried to illustrate in the three commercial strips I have drawn." He graduated from college in 1930 and married his high school sweetheart. His plans for getting rich by way of his drawing were stimulated by the "arrival of new bride and depression on scene at same time." As the depression worsened he lost his newspaper job. He and Sickles opened a commercial art studio together in Columbus, but the business didn't exactly thrive. "At the height of the depression back in 1931 when Milt got canned from his *Columbus Dispatch* job and his morale had hit a new nadir," recalled one of his Sigma Chi brothers, "Milt wrote us offering to become art editor of the *Magazine of Sigma Chi* at $150 per month." There was no room there; Caniff's morale continued to dip. Then came an offer from AP in New York. In those days the local AP office managers acted as talent scouts. The Columbus AP man—Caniff still remembers his name, which was Brophy—had been sending clips of Caniff's stuff back East. Caniff turned the art studio over to Sickles and accepted the proferred job. "Like many another young, ambitious and lightly paid staff man, I was willing to do almost any amount of work to build a name and a bank account," Caniff recalls. "At one point while ostensibly hired as a staff general-assignment man by the syndicate, I was writing and illustrating a four-line, daily, single-column jingle called 'Puffy the Pig,' a three-column panel called 'The Gay Thirties,' a six-column strip, and ghosting another daily and Sunday strip at night." Caniff also did spot illustrations for AP's serialized fiction, political caricatures, and a *Major Hoople*-type panel named *Mr. Gilfeather*. Most of this, except for the ghosting of *Dumb Dora* for his friend Bill Dwyer, was done for the weekly AP salary.

It was that six-column daily adventure strip which changed things. Although Caniff had been sending in sample strips since college, nothing had sold so far. The AP offered a blanket feature service similar to NEA's, with a full page of daily strips available to subscribing clients. After Caniff had been in the bullpen some months, he learned there was a blank space coming up in the page

127

of strips. Political cartoonist Bruce Russell had been trying a humor feature, *Rollingstone*, under the pen name of Bruce Barr and had apparently concluded that comic-strip work was not his métier. "There's going to be a hole," Caniff told himself. He volunteered to fill it. Over a weekend he came up with about a week's samples of a cartoon-style adventure strip. This was *Dickie Dare*, and AP bought it. The original format, the first thing that came to mind according to Caniff, had the twelve-year-old Dickie imagining himself into adventures in various classic adventure stories—*Robin Hood*, *Robinson Crusoe*, and so forth. "Introducing Dickie Dare, sidekick of the world's heroes! A red-blooded modern boy who zooms on the magic carpet of his imagination into the thrills of the glamorous past," explained an introductory strip. After a few months of the glamorous past Caniff found he was losing papers. Figuring it was because his readers already knew the punchlines of the famous public-domain stories he was adapting, he decided to create more suspense by making up his own stories and setting them in the present. Early in May of 1934 Dickie ends a faraway imaginary adventure with Captain Kidd. He's been sitting in the public library. The librarian taps him on the shoulder and tells him it's time to go home. Caniff tells his readers, "His next adventure is to be a surprise for him and you!" The following week, after Dickie, probably expressing Caniff's regrets, has complained, "Nobody seems to understand what fun it is to pal around with guys in history," a new character is introduced. The new man on the job is Dan Flynn, "who is as swashbuckling as any of your story book friends." Flynn is a big, blond, pipe-smoking man, a vagabond author who travels "around the world writing stories of his adventures." When Dan announces to Dickie, "I want you to come with me on a trip around the world!!" Dickie replies, "Hoo-ray!" Dickie's parents have introduced him to Dan in hopes it will bring the dreamy boy back to reality. The advent of Dan Flynn not only brought Dickie closer to reality, it brought Caniff back. He had now arrived at the right vehicle for his assorted talents. The form is still rough, there are too many "Hoo-rays!", but he's getting nearer to *Terry and the Pirates*.

Now that Caniff had an adventure strip of his own and a New York City outlet for it, first the *Post* and then the *Sun*, he attracted more attention. John T. McCutcheon, a Sigma Chi since 1887 and a political cartoonist on the *Chicago Tribune* since 1903, had been touting Caniff to Captain Patterson. So had Walter Berndt, who

Terry was still pretty much a blond Dickie Dare in 1935, and the villains lacked the sophistication of later threats. © 1935 Chicago Tribune–New York News Syndicate, Inc. Reprinted by permission.

was the captain's chief talent scout. More influential in convincing Patterson to get hold of Caniff were the sons of Mollie Slott. She was the assistant general manager of the Trib-News syndicate, and her boys were fans of *Dickie Dare*. After they called her attention to it, Mollie Slott started cutting the strip out. She eventually brought Patterson a batch to look at. Again there was an impending gap to help Caniff's cause. The syndicate's attempts to sell a daily *Teenie Weenies* strip had not been successful, and it was about to be dropped. Something livelier was needed to replace it, maybe something along the lines of *Dickie Dare*. Captain Patterson had Caniff in for a talk. He asked him to try an adventure strip, although he never directly stated he wanted an imitation of *Dickie*. Patterson suggested the action take place in China, then thought to be one of the last outposts of romance, and that it involve pirates. The captain mentioned a couple of books which might inspire the young cartoonist, one was about Chinese pirates and the other was *Wuthering Heights*. The pirates were easy enough to utilize; it took a while longer to work in the unrequited-love plot. "I have never been to China, so I go to the next best place, the Public Library," Caniff has said. "From its picture file, and with careful clipping of every scrap of data on things Oriental, combined with the Encyclopedia Britannica, I am able to piece together a pretty fair background of Far Eastern Lore. For authentic speech mannerisms I plow through a pile of books by traveled people from Pearl Buck to Noel Coward. By now I am an armchair Marco Polo and tipping my hat to every Chinese laundryman in New York." Caniff, as indicated, put a great deal of effort into his new samples. Because, once he'd talked to Patterson, "I knew now I was shooting for the big money."

"Introducing TERRY and the PIRATES," announced the first panel in the very first daily in October 1934. "Terry is a wide awake American boy whose grandfather left him a map of an abandoned mine in China." Accompanying wide-awake young Terry through this simple plot will be Pat Ryan, "two fisted adventurer," George Webster Confucius, "better known as Connie," plus pretty Dale Scott and her crusty father, who bore the inevitable name of Ol' Pop. In order to live up to the new strip's name, Caniff included in the cast a gang of Chinese river pirates, headed by Poppy Joe, "a half-caste who has learned of the treasure." This introductory strip had a wide-open cartoony appearance, seeming to indicate Caniff was going to forget what he'd learned on *Dickie Dare* and make his new feature fit more into the Trib-News pattern as laid down by Chester Gould, Zack Mosley, and their colleagues. The first few weeks, as Terry and Pat arrive in China and venture up-river in quest of the hidden treasure, tended to confirm this notion. Caniff had ghosted *Dumb Dora* a few months earlier, and these dailies give the impression Caniff was still spiritually on campus and not in the Orient. Be that as it may, the syndicate was enthusiastic about *Terry*. They took full-page ads in the trades to extol the new strip. "An exciting new comic is creating a furore in the Chicago Tribune and the New York News! Against a fascinating Oriental locale, Terry and the Pirates is sounding a top note in the adventure field. Its surefire theme . . . makes this new comic a circulation winner anywhere." Actually the feature didn't take hold immediately; some months passed before Caniff knew it was definitely successful.

130

In fact, the *Chicago Tribune* itself didn't pick *Terry* up until its third week.

During his first year in the Orient, Caniff had separate continuities going in his Sunday page. In the first Sunday adventure, Pat and Terry are sailing along the China coast in a steamer "laden with a rich cargo." Sure enough, in keeping with the title, the steamer is captured by pirates. And this batch of sinister Asiatic brigands is not led by a man. "Luvva pete," exclaims Terry, "we're captured by a WOMAN!" Yes, it's the Dragon Lady, making her debut on December 16, 1934, delivering these lines, "So! It is Amelican gentleman who resists so brashly—I am no su'plised!" Besides speaking movie Chinese, the Dragon Lady is noticeably flat-chested. Gradually both her diction and her bosom improve. "Why not . . . make the Number One menace a woman?" Caniff recalls asking himself at the time he was inventing his cast. "One who combines all the best features of past mustache twirlers with the lure of a handsome wench. There was a woman pirate along the China Coast at one time, so it isn't beyond reality. She's fabulously wealthy. Lai Choi San means 'Mountain of Wealth.' That's too much for readers to remember. Call her that once to establish the atmosphere, but the Occidentals have nicknamed her The Dragon Lady."

After the Dragon Lady, Caniff brought in a villain straight out of the silent serials. A chap in a black robe and death's-head mask who actually called himself the Skull. About this point Caniff must have had to make some kind of decision as to whether he would keep Terry the luvva Pete kind of hero of boys' fiction or let him grow up. Fortunately Noel Sickles was again sharing a studio with him; the things Sickles was trying on *Scorchy Smith* began to stimulate Caniff. "My job was not dull, but it consumed the physically available day," Caniff has said. "It was not until Noel Sickles . . . worked out a means of delivering illustration quality pictures on a seven-day basis was I able to buck some of the chains of the working schedule while dramatically improving the all-over value of Terry." It's obvious, when looking over the dailies and Sundays of 1935, that Sickles gave more than advice and inspiration to *Terry and the Pirates*. Many of the panels, especially the long shots of ships, artillery, and planes, were rendered by Sickles. Caniff used the pen less and less, switched to the brush and the liberal use of black. He gave much more attention to the staging of his events and, like Sickles, made use of motion-picture approaches. What he now dis-

Things were looking better in 1937. A trade ad for the strip.

covered for himself had been done by Griffith in the movies twenty years earlier. Caniff moved his camera, liberated the point of view. He introduced long shots, close-ups, boom shots. He became infected with a curiosity similar to Sickles's. What did a train look like from a hundred feet directly above it? What was the difference between the light of early morning and that of midday? Comparing *Terry* and *Scorchy* from the middle 1930s, you can see both men tackling the same problems. There are sequences in both strips, for example, where the only light source in the room is a single overhead lamp.

132

By the end of 1935 Caniff had mastered the impressionist technique; there was very little he couldn't draw. But there were plots he could no longer use. A villain like the Skull was okay for the old cartoon approach, maybe even an Oriental who said, "Amelican." With the sophisticated illustrative style, though, the mustache-twirling sequences didn't fit. So Caniff was obliged to bring his stories up to match the quality of his drawing. Again he used the movies for inspiration, this time borrowing from the A-features turned out by MGM, Paramount, and Warners. "When people flock into a movie or rave about last night's television show, you should know *why* and be ready to work some of that sure-fire entertainment appeal into your feature," Caniff has advised aspiring cartoonists. "When you start noticing how a good scene is built up to its climax, how a comedian leaves them laughing . . . you are educating yourself for cartooning. The tricks of the theater are also the tricks of our branch of entertainment." There were some very good people making movies in the thirties, people whose tricks Caniff adapted to his purposes: directors such as Josef von Sternberg—his 1932 *Shanghai Express* with Marlene Dietrich and Warner Oland could have been story-boarded by Caniff; Tay Garnett, whose 1935 *China Seas* has Gable, Harlow, ships, and piracy as well as the mix of action and comedy that became a *Terry* trademark; Alfred Hitchcock, as interested in chases, bright dialogue, and extended suspense as Caniff himself. Actors, too, were important. Big Stoop was a caricature of the Karloff monster. The Dragon Lady could have been played by the Dietrich of the von Sternberg epics. Sandhurst, the recurrent weakling villain, was based on Charles Laughton. Burma, who came along in 1936, was Caniff's version of the wise, brassy blonde Jean Harlow and Carole Lombard went in for. Burma also owes something to the Joan Crawford version of *Rain*. In the 1932 film Sadie Thompson spends a good many rainy afternoons in her room listening to the "St. Louis Blues" on her windup phonograph. This song was Burma's favorite, always heard before the blonde reappears. When I asked Caniff if he remembered seeing the movie, he replied, "I stole the whole character from Sadie Thompson."

Caniff had a good deal of fun in the middle thirties living up to the subtitle of the strip. He worked every sort of pirate into the stories, from the suave sea-going Judas to the blustering land pirate and smuggler Captain Blaze. Burma herself, as a result of having been Judas's mistress, is wanted for piracy by the British police in

Noel Sickles admits to having a hand in this very cinematic 1938 Sunday page. He also, by the way, designed the Terry logo. © 1938 News Syndicate Co., Inc. Reprinted by permission.

Hong Kong. This kept her moving in and out of the strip. Caniff has frequently used the word *picaresque* in describing his work. *Terry* is certainly a picaresque novel, not in the tradition of *Gil Blas* but closer to the variations worked out by Fielding and Dickens. Pat and Terry are always on the move, on the road. The major villains and secondary characters are continually reappearing, many times in new guises. Caniff also worked in the unrequited-love theme by having Pat fall in love with Normandie Drake during the strip's second year. They are kept apart by the girl's relatives. She later marries the cowardly Sandhurst. Normandie was thereafter woven in and out of the story for the next several years, as was her miserable husband.

Caniff says he wasn't influenced by Captain Patterson as to what to do with the strip, but he did allow his characters to age, marry, have children, and, as with Raven Sherman, die. Similar things, at the suggestion of Patterson, had been going on in several other Trib-News comics. By having Terry go through adolescence and into manhood, Caniff provided himself with a wider range of story possibilities. Terry fell for April Kane, had a crush on Burma, eventually romanced the Dragon Lady. Caniff used sexual motivations more than any of his contemporaries. And because the comics, like the movies then, couldn't be too explicit, he made circumspection into a virtue and built up tension by suggesting rather than showing. Along the way he dealt with some unusual—for comic strips anyway—sexual types, among them the lesbian Sanjak, whose interest in April Kane is used to move the story, and the nymphomaniac Cheery Blaze, whose failure with Pat Ryan prompts her to betray him. Caniff was good, too, at depicting bitchy women. He introduced Nastalthia Smythe-Heatherstone in 1938. She was a child then, a sort of midget Bette Davis. Nastalthia reappears years later, fully grown, and nasty as ever. It was in the use of these characters, and all the sundry males, that Caniff excelled. His theater experience and his love of the movies made him aware of the value of second leads and minor characters. Pat Ryan could have changed places with Scorchy Smith, but there was never in Sickles's strip anyone like Judas, Chopstick Joe, Big Stoop, Klang, April, and the others. Sickles had perfected the strip that was a joy to look at. Caniff made you care about the people he was drawing.

His dedication to authenticity got Caniff into the war against Japan several years ahead of anyone else in the United States. The China he was using in *Terry* was much closer to the real China in the late 1930s than it had been when little knickered Terry had arrived with his treasure map. In the real China they had been fighting a Japanese invasion army since 1937; by 1939 there were 1,000,000 Japanese troops in China. Caniff felt he had to show some of what was going on in his adopted country in *Terry and the Pirates*. He started mentioning the invaders in the spring of 1938, by having the Dragon Lady recruit a guerilla army to fight against them. Soon invader planes were appearing in the sky, battlefields became part of the scenery. Caniff backed off from the war for some months, finishing up the year with a story set in what was then French Indochina. He couldn't ignore the war in China, though, and from the end of 1939 on the stories were almost all concerned with the invaders. Caniff told me his introduction of the Japanese into his strip caused one of the few conflicts he ever had with Patterson. As an active supporter of Roosevelt, Caniff was considerably to the left of the captain and even further from Colonel McCormick. This never caused him trouble, but Patterson did get upset when he saw Japanese soldiers in *Terry*. He indicated that such unpleasant elements as war did not properly belong in a comic strip. Caniff disagreed. Patterson kept grumbling until Pearl Harbor, but he never directly ordered a change.

The wartime *Terry* seems a little too gung ho and somewhat oversimple in its attitudes when looked at today. At the time, with an incredible anti-Japanese feeling in the country (which resulted in such things as the internment of Japanese-Americans in concentration camps), Caniff's views were moderate. "Neither unbelievably clever nor incredibly stupid, they are probably a good deal like real Japs," observed the *New Yorker* in 1944 in discussing his handling of the invaders. "Caniff has even let them win a few battles."

When the war ended, Caniff knew he was going to be giving up his characters. He was earning about $70,000 a year from *Terry*. Marshall Field and the Chicago Sun Syndicate offered him a guaranteed $2,000 per week for five years—plus, which was more important, ownership of his characters—if he'd come up with a new comic strip. Caniff agreed to the deal. His last year of *Terry and the Pirates* was 1946, and it contains some of his best work. Terry, though still connected with the Air Force, is posing as a mercenary pilot and flying for Chopstick Joe. Like the final chapter of a Victorian picaresque, the last months of *Terry* brought back all sorts of scattered characters. The Dragon Lady, Burma, Captain Blaze, Jane Allen all show up again. Like the last scenes of a movie Caniff

It's 1939, and Caniff is at war. Even when strung up, the Dragon Lady manages to be epigrammatic in the best Ching Chow tradition. © 1939 by News Syndicate Co., Inc. Reprinted by permission.

ended with pictures and no dialogue. The final Sunday shows Terry saying goodbye to Jane Allen at a snow-covered airfield. She starts for the plane, runs back to him, there is a clinch, and then she's on the plane and flying away into the fading day. Terry turns away from us toward his waiting jeep, passing a New Year's party poster. It says, "Ring out the old, ring in the new."

Caniff's next-to-last month on Terry. Burma is about to make her final farewell appearance. © *1946 News Syndicate Co., Inc. Reprinted by permission.*

Chapter 8
Gloryosky!

KIDS AND VIOLENCE were teamed in comics from the beginning, but at first it was all for laughs. A good many of the earliest features were about kids—*The Yellow Kid, The Katzenjammer Kids, Little Jimmy, Buster Brown, The Kin-Der-Kids, Little Nemo.* Usually the funny-paper child in those remote days was a brat and a prankster, akin to the mischief-makers of the school-daze vaudeville skits. The pages were aimed at the kids themselves, providing them with a few chuckles and a four-color working out of their dreams of revenge on the grown-up world. As the twentieth century grew older, the people in the comic-strip business learned a few things. They discovered, for instance, that the grown-ups themselves were reading the funnies. They also found out, after noticing the lines in front of the new movie palaces, that all kinds of people would pay to be entertained by stories about children.

The most convincing proof of this was the career of Mary Pickford. In movies since the first decade of the century, she was by 1916 earning $10,000 a week. She remained "America's sweetheart" for over twenty years, retiring as one of the richest women in America. What had brought Mary Pickford, and her movie studios, such huge amounts of money were films in which she portrayed

children. "When she had reached twenty and stood ready to im-
personate young love, Famous Players began to cast her as a child.
It was an immediate and furious hit," says Will Irwin in his biography of Zukor. "Put her in pinafores and she was eight years old
again. She stood and walked and managed her head like a child;
she even held her hands like a child." Mary Pickford played every
sort of child, from Pollyanna to Little Lord Fauntleroy, and plucky
orphans were her specialty. "To hold her lead, she always had to play
Little Mary, a girl on the verge of puberty," observed Richard
Griffith and Arthur Mayer in *The Movies*. "Yet always hovering in
the wings was a male admirer, frequently elderly, and the im-
plication dangled that someday, beyond the final fade-out, perhaps . . ." The basic ingredients of Mary Pickford's films and character engendered, as we'll see shortly, a good many kid adventure
strips from the 1920s onward. Another influential screen child was
Jackie Coogan, who for a few years, after appearing with Chaplin
in *The Kid*, was another of America's little millionaire sweet-
hearts.

So gradually a new sort of kid character took to the comic pages,
a kid who owed something to the Horatio Alger tradition, something to the newer pulp-adventure magazines, and a good deal to
the movies of Mary Pickford and Jackie Coogan. These serious, or
at least semi-serious, strips were of two basic kinds: those utilizing waifs and orphans, and those given to the feats of heroic young
boys. We'll scrutinize the orphans first.

The all-time champion of the waifs is Little Orphan Annie.
Heartland born, Harold Gray found his way to Chicago and a position
in the *Tribune* art department. "One strip I feel indirectly to have
had a tiny part in was *Little Orphan Annie*," longtime *New Yorker*
artist Garrett Price told me. "My friend from Purdue, Harold Gray,
and I lived with the same private family in Chicago. We had afternoon and evening jobs in the art department of the *Chicago
Tribune*. Mornings we played tennis. Harold got fired. One day Sid
Smith asked me if I would assist him with Andy Gump. My ambition was to be an illustrator and I declined. Did I know anybody he
could get? Yes, Harold Gray." Price rightly believes that the five
years Gray served with *The Gumps* taught him almost everything
he needed to know about how to fashion a successful strip. It's also
probable that Captain Patterson contributed to the creation of
Little Orphan Annie, since he was a firm believer in the movies as
a barometer of mass public taste. "He used to go to the movies, and

watch very closely what the audience laughed at, what they liked and didn't like," Walter Berndt remembers about Patterson. "Whenever he saw something that the audiences reacted to enthusiastically, he put that in the *News*." The *Orphan Annie* strip, in its relatively unpolitical early days, was a composite of the most successful Mary Pickford films. There was the tough little orphan lass taken into the palatial home, her back-talking and joke-playing and her slangy honesty, and there was the gruff millionaire (Daddy Warbucks in his first rough-edged version) who becomes her mentor and protector. And that squiggly mass of hair Gray endowed Annie with looks like an attempt, albeit clumsy, to imitate the Mary Pickford curls so many millions of people were in love with still when the strip made its debut in August of 1924.

Gray drew only a shade better than Sidney Smith. The public didn't seem to care. It was the characters and the stories they bought. "In the office *Little Orphan Annie* was anything but popular," recalls Garrett Price. "At the first opportunity it was left out of the paper. The *Tribune* was bombarded with phone calls, all of which could not have been made by Harold. From then on *Orphan Annie* was pushed; and it never faltered." Gray always remained ambivalent toward his red-haired, blank-eyed heroine. Quite obviously he enjoyed the endless dismal predicaments he thrust her into, and relished the chance in the New Deal years to use his strip as a soapbox from which he could heckle FDR and all the liberal notions loose in the nation. In most interviews and public statements, though, he tried to disarm his critics by himself attacking the foolish aspects of the strip. He referred to Annie as "our loveable little monster," and in explaining her beginnings he said, "In those days she was *East Lynne, Over the Hill to the Poorhouse* and all the other favorites rolled into one and modernized. She was not a 'comic.' Life to her was deadly serious." In 1947 Gray did a sequence about Tik Tok, a cartoonist who becomes famous with a strip called *Little Widget the Waif.* Gray had been turning out Annie's adventures for almost a quarter of a century by then and apparently did not think too kindly of waifs, the cartoonist's life, or the fans of comic strips. When Annie helps Tik Tok go over his fan mail, she finds the letters are either pleas for handouts or attacks on the cartoonist: "You dirty fascist moron! You sadistic swine! The funny paper should be funny! Ain't there enough sadness in the world?" Meeting readers up close is even worse. Walking with Annie and the ever-present Sandy, Tik Tok encounters a sobbing, unkempt lout

It's a mean old world, even for the successful creator of a waif strip. Espe-cially if the world is Harold Gray's. © 1947 Chicago Tribune-New York News Syndicate, Inc. Reprinted by permission.

who is reading his strip in the newspaper. "Look! That poor little tyke! Never hurt a soul! And that big thug broke her arm! Why? Why must such things be? . . . I'll beat th' ears off'n that guy that done that to poor Little Widget!" Gray's epigraph for this particular Sunday page is, "Ah, fame! It's wonderful, so they say . . . But when you step suddenly into that spotlight, pal, be ready to duck." Harold Gray stayed in the spotlight until his death in 1968, aided on the strip by Bob Leffingwell for several decades. The ill-suited team of Tex Blaisdell and Elliot Caplin took over thereafter and succeeded, on the strength of Blaisdell's inept artwork and Caplin's clumsy scripts, in lowering the circulation steadily year by year. After they quit, artists and writers of increasing inability struggled with *Annie*, the last being a boy who drew with a felt marker and tried to turn Gray's waif into a liberal. In 1974 the syndicate concluded that only Gray could do justice to *Little Orphan Annie,* so they un-earthed his old proofs and began reprinting his work from forty years before.

Jay Jerome Williams, in the middle twenties, turned to a more venerable waif tradition for his inspiration. The strips he wrote borrowed from the numerous pluck-and-luck, onward-and-upward novels which Horatio Alger, Jr., had ground out in the nineteenth century. He was relatively open about where he was getting his ideas, going so far as to use the pen name Edwin Alger on both *Phil Hardy* and *Bound to Win.* Williams was a newspaperman and later a radio commentator. His *Phil Hardy,* which began at the end of 1925, dealt with a plucky lad who runs away to sea. The artist was George Storm, embarking on his first nationally syndicated strip. After *Phil Hardy* sank, Williams came up with *Bound to Win.* This one proved sturdier, managing to thrive from the late 1920s through the 1930s. The hero was an adolescent who wandered from adventure to adventure accompanied by "his faithful dog, Briar." Ben was not your ragged shortpants hero; he always appeared in a suit and tie with his hair neatly brushed. Nobody except Edwin Alger ever got a credit on the strip, which eventually ran daily and Sunday. Several artists depicted Ben's strivings for upward mobility, mostly undistinguished chaps attempting to imitate their betters. The weekend version was called *Ben Webster's Page*. It dealt initially with the lives of famous men, then switched to adventure continuities. The cartoonist on the final years of *Ben Webster* Sundays (older comic-book readers may remember seeing the pages reprinted in *All-American Comics*) seems to have been a Florida artist named Calvin Fader. Many of these later Sunday stories departed from the work-and-win ethic to fool with fantasy and science fiction themes. By 1940 Ben's winning streak was over.

Graduating from the Edwin Alger stable, George Storm went into business with a waif of his own. The lad's name was Bobby Thatcher; his adventures began appearing on the daily comic pages in March of 1927. "Bobby Thatcher, a bright lad of fourteen, lives on a farm near the village of Lakeview. He is the ward of Jed Flint, and lives with Flint and his housekeeper," Storm tells his readers by way of introduction. "Since the death of Mrs. Flint, who was kind to him, Bobby no longer attends school and his life is one of increasing hardship." Bobby's chief hardship is old Flint, as hard a man as his name implies. Flint overworks the boy ("When I was a lad I didn't lay abed till four in the morning"), scorns his ambitions ("If it ain't one fool notion it's another . . . get that notion of school outa your head"), appropriates any outside money he earns ("I'll just put this money by for you till you're twenty one"), beats him, locks him in the attic, and in general behaves in the accepted stepfather-guardian manner. Bobby, of course, runs away before the strip is two weeks old ("I'll hate to leave—it's the only home I've ever known"). Storm now adds some contemporary touches to Bobby's odyssey. The boy hitches a ride from a stranger in a powerful touring car. The helpful stranger, it turns out, is wanted by the sheriff and the state troopers. A chase, including a race to beat a screaming locomotive to a grade crossing, ensues. What Storm is doing is mixing movie excitement with his Horatio Alger story line. He continued to do this throughout the strip's run, alternating babies left in wicker baskets on doorsteps with surly rum-runners blasting

Horatio Alger meets the movies. Two early samples of George Storm's Bobby Thatcher. © 1927 McClure Newspaper Syndicate. Reprinted by permission.

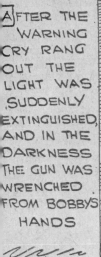

away with tommy guns. Bobby's picaresque wanderings through the 1920s and 1930s exposed him to almost every kind of adventure format—aviation, detective, cowboy, seafaring, you name it.

Although *Bobby Thatcher* has been virtually forgotten, and is not even discussed in any of the published books on the comics, it was a very popular and successful strip. In 1929 the McClure Syndicate boasted, in trade ads, that it was "the strongest boy strip published . . . Holds the record for growth and holding power." A lengthy and impressive list of client papers, topped by the *New York World,* was furnished. Storm moved his creation to the Bell Syndicate in 1930, where it continued to thrive. As the thirties progressed, and bigger and better violence hit the funny papers, the syndicate emphasized the homespun, decent quality of the action and excitement in *Bobby Thatcher.* More than likely this was an indication Storm's brand of sentimental adventure was finding less favor with newspaper readers. In the spring of 1937 Storm gave the handling of the strip back to the McClure people. He seems to have lost interest in *Bobby* at this point, finding he no longer had enough enthusiasm to draw it. "I think by that time it had become drudgery to him," Sheldon Mayer told me. Mayer, who'd been haunting newspapers and syndicates since he was fourteen, was then working as a combined editor-writer-cartoonist at McClure's. He had just turned twenty when the job of ghosting the strip fell to him. Storm had always done all of his drawing and writing himself, so there was no assistant to fill in until he got back in the mood to turn out *Bobby Thatcher* again. Mayer, a longtime admirer of Storm's work, was elated. Each week he got to travel out to Long Island and get Storm's approval on the strips he'd penciled. "Storm had an eight-room house in Southport, an attic studio, a sailboat, a pretty wife, and a quiet life," Mayer recalls. Mayer was already doing a comic-book feature about a boy cartoonist named Scribbly, dreaming of a syndicated strip of his own. To him Storm's life-style was something to aim for. Storm, however, simply couldn't get back to work on the strip. He let it die. "The strip was still grossing about $250 a week. . . . Storm's cut of it, even after I was paid, was about $100 a week. A substantial salary at that time, but I guess he was used to more." Storm sold his house, moved to Oklahoma where he and his wife took up residence on a farm. Mayer thinks maybe Storm had the cartoonist's equivalent of the seven-year itch, ten in his case, and had to get away from *Bobby Thatcher.*

It was through Sheldon Mayer that Storm, at the end of the thirties, got back into cartooning. By that time Mayer had joined his McClure boss, M. C. Gaines, in producing a line of comic books. Their first titles were *All-American* and *Flash*. The earliest issues of *All-American* reprinted some *Bobby Thatcher* sequences. In the first number of *Flash Comics* Storm tried his hand at a more serious approach to cartooning and drew a Zorro-like hero known as the Whip. Apparently he also had hopes of getting back into syndication with another boy adventure strip. This one was *Danny Magee*, complete with put-upon farmboy and flint-hearted guardian. It ended up, briefly, in a comic book. The next few years George Storm worked chiefly in comic books. He changed jobs as frequently as his footloose waif, working a few months for almost every publisher in the early forties. He drew humorous fillers, serious super-heroes, anything. His credits for those years include *The Hangman*, *Bugs Bunny*, *The Black Owl*, *Colonel Porterhouse*, *Ty-Gor*, *The Flying Trio*, and many more. He did manage to work on at least two more newspaper strips, both already established features. He ghosted a few weeks of *Joe Jinks* in the fall of 1940, took over *The Adventures of Patsy* in 1943 for a short run. After the war supermen went into one of their periodic declines; true crime and funny stuff became popular. Storm came up with a somewhat anachronistic teenager named Buzzy. Soon there was a *Buzzy* comic book. Commenting on his new success at the time, Storm said, "Last two or three years my work has become popular again. May be making a comeback. They say if you stick around long enough hoopskirts and derbies come back into style." True to pattern, though, Storm dropped *Buzzy* after a year or so. His work showed up in less and less prestigious publications until the early 1950s.

While the writing on *Bobby Thatcher* was mostly conventional, the drawing was quirky and original. Storm's first professional cartooning was done in San Francisco for the *News* in the early twenties. His style then was very much in the big-foot tradition, resembling the sort of thing being taught by the less imaginative mail-order schools. He next went through a spell of imitating the still-prominent John T. McCutcheon. Then suddenly, when he undertook the *Phil Hardy* strip in 1925, he was working in the sprawling, scratchy style which he stuck with for the rest of his life. His work had an easy-going tenseness, a sort of casual power. Sometimes, when Storm seems to have been rushing a job, all the quality goes and only a hurried scribbling remains. Nobody else ever drew quite like him at his best, though.

Nineteen twenty-seven was a vintage year for waifs and orphans, especially over at the Hearst works. King Features introduced them in batches, offering both *Little Annie Rooney* and a strip with the no-nonsense title of *Two Orphans*. This latter one was the work of Al Zère, a man with several short-run features to his credit. Covering all the bases, Zère peopled his strip with one little girl orphan, one little boy orphan, and a dog. True to the Harold Gray tradition, both little Tess and little Bub had no pupils in their eyes. The dog didn't either. Despite all this, *Two Orphans* did not last long. *Little Annie Rooney* had better luck.

The link with motion-picture moppets is somewhat more direct here. Mary Pickford had made a movie called *Little Annie Rooney* in 1925. Tom McNamara, who was associated with the Pickford organization in the middle twenties, once told me he'd tried to interest King Features in a comic-strip *Annie Rooney* while the movie was in production. He wrote samples, getting Bud Counihan to do the drawing. King was not interested at the time. McNamara always maintained that the 1927 comic strip was a swipe of his original pitch. In spite of this setback, McNamara became something of an orphan expert. He worked on the first *Little Orphan Annie* talkie in the early thirties.

The first artist to draw *Little Annie Rooney* signed himself Verd. His name was Ed Verdier, and he worked in a simple, uncluttered, cartoon style. Annie was a feisty kid in those days, much better looking than Gray's orphan but close to her in her wisecracking approach to life's pitfalls. In the first sequence she is living with her old Uncle Bob, and a crooked lawyer named Scringe is trying to do her out of her grandfather's fortune. By 1930 Annie Rooney had wandered a lot, had even put in some time working with a circus, and was being looked after by Aunt Aggie and Uncle Paddy, an overwhelmingly good-hearted pair. Annie switched artists almost as frequently as surrogate parents. She began the thirties being rendered by Ben Batsford, whose work was more nervous and noodled than Verd's. Batsford's Annie was still a spunky kid ("That's a lotta carrot oil!"), little realizing the tidal wave of treacle was about to engulf her. She next fell into the hands of Brandon Walsh and Darrel McClure, the team who were to have their way with her throughout the thirties and forties.

"Gee, Zero, I got the wim-wams awful bad. I keep tryin' to pretend I ain't scared of Mrs. Meany, but I know I am. An' I kin tell by the way Uncle George looks that he is worrying 'bout something, too. . . . If I ain't here Uncle George kin help that nice prince who saved his life an' I kin go someplace where Mrs. Meany can't find me—I kin tell Uncle George I'm gonna stay with Mrs. Cleanly at the laundry . . . " Zero was Annie's bedraggled mutt, surely the most long-suffering animal in comics. Silver had to put up with a lot of "Hi Yo, Silver!", but poor Zero had to listen to all those monologues of Annie's. She talked to him night and day, across whole and entire Sunday pages. "Don't worry, Zero—it ain't snowing very hard. This is a big city—an' I'll betcha I get a job someplace—besides, we have over sixty-cents, so we don't have to be hungry!" When she wasn't being aggressively optimistic or suffering from recurrent bouts of the wim-wams, Little Annie Rooney was in a euphoric state of happiness wherein she would exclaim, "Gloryosky!" For example: "Gloryosky, Zero, you look grand! Honest, you do tricks like pooches in the circus!" She was on the run for all of the thirties, eluding "heartless, cruel Mrs. Meany," her legal guardian. The continuities were a paranoid's delight, for no matter how well Annie did or how prominent were her temporary parents, Mrs. Meany would always track her down. "I'd do anything to get my hands on that little brat!" she often exclaimed. Time didn't help Annie either; there was no chance of the usual escape from an unhappy childhood. Annie remained forever on the brink of puberty; Mrs. Meany remained her wrinkled harpy self.

The plots and dialogue were by Walsh. As we saw earlier, he'd been employed to fashion predicaments for the Gump family especially little Chester. According to King Features publicity, Walsh had been writing *Little Annie Rooney* since 1928. If this is true, something must have happened to him when Darrel McClure joined him, possibly a bad case of the wim-wams. Annie lost all of her spunk and feistiness at that point. McClure had drawn several other things for King prior to Annie. These included *Hard-Hearted Hicky* and *Vanilla and the Villains,* both written by Harry Hershfield and both parodies of the hapless orphan-mustached villain melodramatics which Walsh took seriously in the *Annie Rooney* saga.

Early in 1934 Nicholas Afonsky was lured away from his job of ghosting the sober and serious *Minute Movie* scenarios. His soulful style was turned loose on the *Little Annie Rooney* Sunday page. McClure was never happy about giving Annie up every seventh day to another artist, even though King Features attempted to pacify him by letting him try a new Sunday page of his own. It was *Donnie*, about a seagoing waif, and it did not last long. Exactly why *Annie* was split between two different artists is not clear. Ed Wheelan contended, as you'll recall, that Afonsky was hired by Hearst as part of the plot against him, and that once the Russian-born artist was sitting around King they had to come up with something for him to do. At any rate, Afonsky kept the Sunday *Annie* until his death in 1943. During his early tenure on the page the little girl rarely appeared, the adventures were concerned with a sweetfaced wandering friend of hers named Joey. Joey's mentor was an epigrammatic Chinese named Ming Foo. Ming Foo spouted the same fortune-cookie philosophy as Ching Chow, the epigrammatic Chinese Walsh had invented for *The Gumps* Sunday pages. "It is wisely written: we weep when we are born and every day explains why," Ming Foo would remark as their airship is about to crash into an iceberg. "On tablets of white jade is inscribed: 'To avoid suffering die young!'" he quips as they are about to go over a waterfall on their raft. Since the fatalistic Oriental didn't have a dog, it was little Joey who had to endure all those aphorisms. Later on in the thirties Ming Foo moved upstairs into a Sunday half-page of his own. Little Annie continued on into the fifties, managing to stay one jump ahead of Mrs. Meany to the end.

Although the great swing to adventure strips came in the 1930s, there was a smaller jump to straight stuff in the late twenties. Some unexpected people switched to derring-do about that time, the most unlikely being Gus Mager. Charles A. "Gus" Mager had been a big-foot man, a member of what the *New York Times* referred to as the "bulb nose" school, for most of the century. His strips about Monks, ape-jawed folks probably derived from the then still current caricature of the Irish immigrant, had appeared in the early days of comic strips. Mager's habit of naming his Monks after their dominant humor—Henpecko, Sherlocko, Groucho, Tightwado—is what inspired the nicknames of the Marx Brothers. After deserting Hearst for the *World*, Mager changed his Sherlocko the Monk into Hawkshaw the detective for a full Sunday page. "A good, thorough-going burlesque of the great detective and . . . rousing entertainment," Coulton Waugh called the feature. Mager abandoned Hawkshaw and his blundering assistant, first called Watso and then the Colonel, to try a family page titled *Main Street*. That didn't succeed. By 1928 Mager was even further from the slapstick of *Hawkshaw*, doing a kid hero strip named

Oliver's Adventures. Oliver, though a loner who owed his name to Dickens's better-known orphan, had more flamboyant adventures than most of the waifs we've encountered so far. Teaming up with aviators and detectives, he devoted most of his time to tangling with South American revolutionaries, wild jungle animals, escaped killers, and the like. His most constant companion was a burly pilot named Captain Breeze, whose gruff looks and broken nose give him some resemblance to Captain Easy, who debuted nearly a year after him. The raspy, heavily black style Mager affected on the *Oliver* strip seems to have been influenced by the work of George Storm. It's like nothing Mager did before or after.

While Gus Mager was still under contract to do *Oliver's Adventures,* his old friend Rudolph Dirks invited him to revive *Hawkshaw the Detective* as a topper to the *Captain and the Kids* Sunday page. Mager agreed, but didn't use his name. He signed the new *Hawkshaw,* which utilized his old bulb-nose style, Watso. For several years thereafter Mager alternated between detective parodies for Sunday and straight adventure for the weekdays. Oliver hung on through 1934, although the strip's name in its final days was *Oliver and His Dog.* Hawkshaw and Watso did better, not closing up shop until after WWII.

After he was bounced off *Little Annie Rooney,* Ben Batsford soon returned with another waif. The unfortunate kid was a boy this time around, a curly-top tyke named Frankie Doodle. Batsford had begun the strip, syndicated by United Features, as *The Doodle Family.* Apparently feeling more comfortable with orphans, he soon killed off everybody but poor Frankie and put the strip in his name. Not only was Frankie Doodle a put-upon orphan, he was, like so many waifs of nineteenth-century novels, "the heir to a great fortune." For a good part of his career, which stretched from the early to late 1930s, Frankie was plagued by a crooked lawyer named Mr. Shady, who wants Frankie's money for his own evil purposes. Probably Frankie's late parents made a mistake in ever trusting a lawyer with a name like that. Even worse than Mr. Shady is Mrs. Krule, who operates the orphanage, run along the lines of Dotheboys Hall, from which Frankie is continually escaping. We should probably feel some compassion for Mrs. Krule, since with a name like hers she undoubtedly couldn't get any other kind of work except orphanage keeping—especially during the depression. Although Frankie never owned a dog to confide in, he did have not one but two epigrammatic Chinese mentors. One was Ming Low, a cook

151

in Chinatown, and the other was Captain Ku, a Chinese secret agent. Frankie first meets the captain when he becomes involved with a sinister waterfront gang known as the Society of the Stinging Wasps. The society is presided over by a woman known only as the Queen, whom Batsford refers to as the foundress of the society. Frankie enjoys this particular adventure, though he is sometimes puzzled by the actions of the secret agent and exclaims at one point, "Gosh! These Chinese detectives are MYSTERIOUS!" Batsford alternated orphanage episodes with adventures set in Chinatown, the North Woods, and the Wild West. *Frankie Doodle* never achieved much in the way of newspaper circulation. However, in the late thirties and early forties, after the strip itself had been discontinued, United reprinted it in *Tip Top Comics*, giving Frankie a larger audience than he had perhaps ever had before.

In the late 1920s some of the gag-a-day kids turned to heroics. When *Freckles and His Friends* started back in 1915, its sole purpose was to deliver a joke every day. Never completely abandoning gags, Merrill Blosser came to rely considerably on adventure continuities from the late twenties onward. Freckles, most often accompanied by his pal Oscar, would leave his small-town schoolroom milieu to ride with cowboys out West, sail to desert islands, fly dangerous missions with daredevil aviators. Blosser kept in competition with his NEA co-worker Roy Crane until the late thirties. Freckles then turned into a teenager, Henry Formhals started ghosting the dailies, and airplanes and six-guns were no more. Smitty, Walter Berndt's office boy, was also a jokesmith when he popped up in 1922. Eventually Berndt added continuity, frequently throwing Smitty into contact with the sports world and real-life heroes like Babe Ruth. In the 1930s, particularly, *Smitty* moved away from the paddock and the diamond to the more standard adventure locations—desert islands, the North Woods, the South Seas. But only on workdays; Sunday was always a joke day.

What Jackie Coogan and Mary Pickford did to comic strips in the twenties, Shirley Temple repeated in the thirties. Pushed into the movies at the age of three, Shirley Temple became a major star before she was six. In 1934 no less than nine of her films were released. The titles of some of her early pictures—*Bright Eyes, Curly Top, Dimples*—indicate what the depression public found so appealing about the little star. Three years running, from 1936 through 1938, she came in first in the *Motion Picture Herald* poll of box-office attractions. She is credited, along with Will Rogers, with sav-

Here's Freckles when his friends were an adventurous lot. It's possible this 1933 daily was actually drawn by Blosser himself. © 1933 NEA. Reprinted by permission.

The Adventures of Patsy

October 19, 1936, and Patsy and her Uncle Phil are about to journey to Hollywood for the first time. The adventures followed her, as we see in the sec-

THE ADVENTURES OF PATSY

ond Mel Graff daily, this one from 1938. © 1936, 1938 AP. Reprinted by permission.

ing the Fox studios from bankruptcy in the middle 1930s. Naturally enough, syndicate editors began thinking about winsome little tots during these same years. This resulted in several new comic strips, the most interesting of which was *The Adventures of Patsy*.

Patsy was introduced by the AP Syndicate in 1934, with Mel Graff as artist. "She was my own idea," Graff told me when I asked him about the beginnings of the feature, "and was supposed to be an *Alice in Wonderland* strip. But it didn't jell, so I worked Patsy into a Temple movie moppet." It took Graff several years to move Patsy from one wonderland to the other. In the opening sequence, done in a very stylized cartoon style, Patsy is carried away to the kingdom of Ods Bodkins by her new kite. There she encounters a colony of small-sized folks ruled over by King Silhouette. There are giants and witches to worry about, too. To pull Patsy and her little-boy sidekick, Thimble, out of the various overly familiar scrapes, Graff introduced the Phantom Magician, a masked and costumed hero. The Phantom, as he is usually called, is soon transformed into Patsy's uncle, Phil Cardigan. By the middle of 1935 Patsy is back to reality, having real-world adventures. Graff began to change his style, obviously under the influence of what had been going on around him at AP in the work of Noel Sickles and the recently graduated Milton Caniff. Graff's previous stuff, on the early *Patsy* and on the thousands of spot drawings he's done since joining AP, had the elongated, patterned look which Russell Patterson and Ralph Barton had made popular in the slick magazines of the twenties. Now heavily brushed in shadows and intricate realistic backgrounds begin to appear.

From 1936 on Graff did some of his most impressive work on *Patsy*. The first continuity in 1936, apparently inspired by J. D. Ratcliff's *And Sudden Death*, concerned highway safety. Uncle Phil is appointed State Commissioner of Public Safety, a job which seems to involve the wearing of a fancy uniform. The story, wherein Patsy is also kidnapped by milk racketeers, is weighted down with propaganda. The drawing, though, is splendid. Graff is now ready to try anything. Like Caniff, and more especially Sickles, he becomes fascinated with the effects of light and shadow. And, like them, he is one of the few adventure-strip artists ever to convey a sense of place and of time, and even a feel of the weather. He would vary scenes of night action in a snowy railroad station with interior shots where the only illumination is a log fire or an oil lamp. Using a simple benday pattern, he drew a nightclub inter-

The ill-fated Charles Raab kept Patsy in the Caniff-Sickles camp, though he gave her a new mentor. © 1941 AP. Reprinted by permission.

lude of several days where the only light comes from small table lamps. Graff continued to experiment throughout the year, trying double-tone rendering, then doing several weeks in a scratchy pen style. He was one of the first to break a day's strip into three instead of four or five panels. That meant, in those days of six-column dailies, he had plenty of room in each panel. His layouts, his selection of shots, and his design sense are commendable. These middle and late 1930s years of *The Adventures of Patsy* contain the best drawing Graff ever did. Even the inadequate reproduction the AP strips got in many of their small-town client papers didn't spoil the strength of the work.

At last, in December of 1936, Patsy and Uncle Phil arrived in Hollywood. Graff did not try, as some of the artists and writers of kid strips did, to make Patsy play the kind of cute, dimpled role Shirley Temple was then undertaking in her films. Instead he made Patsy an actress, embroiling her in the relatively real side of Shirley Temple's life. "I never did live in Hollywood," Graff told me, "though many studios sent me slick action photos." His Hollywood has that larger-than-life fantasy feel of all imagined locales. There are palm trees sprouting everywhere, everybody seems to live in a ranch-style house. Inside the movie studios you can't take a step without bumping into a huge movie camera, a bank of lights, or a flock of extras. The Hollywood adventures were balanced between behind-the-scenes stories of old actors trying to make comebacks and headstrong young directors being reconciled with their wives and families, and kidnapping and hijacking interludes with gangsters and escaped cons. There was also some kidding of the motion-picture world, particularly when Patsy's Goldwynesque producer, J. P. Panberg of Paragon Pictures, was on the scene. Mel Graff stayed with *Patsy* until 1940 when he got the nod from King Features to take over *Secret Agent X-9*.

The next artist was Charles Raab. Raab had been a classmate and fraternity brother of Milton Caniff at Ohio State, and had assisted both Caniff and Alfred Andriola. Commencing drawing *The Adventures of Patsy* in a tight version of the Andriola *Charlie Chan* style, Raab soon adopted a choppy, thick, black approach. He may have been influenced by Noel Sickles, who was giving him advice on how to handle the strip and also ghosting it on occasion. Phil Cardigan was in New York when Raab started, and he kept him offstage. He brought on a lean, ugly, out-of-work agent named Skidd to look after Patsy and to serve the uncle function. Although he was sloppy and much more inclined to swipe than his peers, Raab always did an interesting job on *Patsy*. He left the strip by 1943, relinquishing it to George Storm. Storm, in turn, gave way to a string of increasingly less talented cartoonists. Raab, meantime, attempted to sell another strip. He tried one called *Foreign Correspondent*, but it, like all his other tries, did not sell. He drifted into comic books in the later forties. Raab's work, none of it signed, showed up in the true-crime comic books of the period, and he even had another crack at Charlie Chan, doing a few stories for the 1948-49 comic book. None of Raab's comic-strip work was ever reprinted in comic books or in histories of the field, and he remains the least known of the artists who worked in the Caniff-Sickles style. And because of his down-and-out end, few of the men who knew him care to talk much about him even now.

Fanny Cory had been a professional children's illustrator for nearly forty years by the time she got into the kid-strip business. Born in 1877, she sold her first drawing to *St. Nicholas* magazine in 1896. She was soon thereafter appearing in *Life*, the *Saturday Evening Post*, and *Scribner's*. By the end of the century she had branched out into children's book illustration. In 1901 she did the pictures for *The Master Key*, the first of several L. Frank Baum books she illustrated. In 1904 Miss Cory, who'd spent part of her growing-up years there, returned to Montana, married, and settled on an eighteen-hundred-acre ranch near Helena. She continued to illustrate children's books, in a style influenced by Howard Pyle, Arthur Rackham, and the art nouveau crowd. In the mid-1920s she and her husband, now with three children ready for college, found they needed something beyond ranching and book illustrating. Fanny Cory, whose brother was a political cartoonist, decided to try the newspaper syndicates. She sold a one-column panel, *Sonnysayings*, to the Philadelphia Ledger Syndicate in 1928. The feature was popular, surviving into the fifties.

Then in 1934 Miss Cory did her first newspaper strip. Also for the Ledger syndicate, this was titled *Babe Bunting*. "Here is HEART INTEREST pitched to its very ultimate," the syndicate announced to prospective buyers. Babe was a curly-haired little tyke, clearly intended to grab the Shirley Temple fans. "The child playing the title role has the very maximum of beauty. This insures 100% more appeal than offered by other children's strips featuring youngsters that are either comic or grotesque." So much for *Orphan Annie*. Babe, another seeming orphan, was initially a salty little thing. Her reaction to patronizing adults is usually, "She's just talking through her hat." The following year Fanny Cory got the call from Hearst and went over to King Features.

Babe was turned over to Roy L. Williams, already in his sixties and a veteran of several decades as a staff artist on newspapers around the country. Williams worked in a stodgy version of the sketchy pen-and-ink style favored by Frank Godwin and most other Ledger cartoonists of the thirties. Babe Bunting became sweeter, acquired the requisite shaggy dog, whom she talked to about life and its problems. Once, when it looked as though Babe might inherit millions, she told her dog that money wasn't very important. "How about you, Buttons? A million bones wouldn't make you any happier? All I want is mother—an' lots of good friends like Mrs. Crumpet—an' enough to eat." The little girl's life was filled with all the paraphernalia of small-town drama—mortgages, lurking hobos, girls cast out into the snow. Before Roy Williams died in 1938, Babe had been reunited with her mother. The strip dragged on for another year, drawn by the reliable Ledger pinch-hitter Kemp Starrett.

Meanwhile, Fanny Cory had been doing another little-girl adventure strip for King Features. This one was named *Little Miss Muffet*, another title inspired by a nursery rhyme and, most likely, also by the Shirley Temple movie of the year preceding the strip's debut, *Little Miss Marker*. The new strip was a moderate success, but Fanny Cory never thought much of it. She had no hand in the writing, which she felt was too bland. "There are no gangsters, or divorces or anything like that in her adventures, so she must be a relief to mothers," she told an interviewer in the late 1930s. "But sometimes I think she's too pure." Nevertheless Miss Cory stayed with the strip. Living alone on her Montana ranch, she continued with *Miss Muffet* until 1956. She died in 1972, five years short of a century old.

When Milton Caniff departed AP for the greener pastures of Captain Patterson, he abandoned *Dickie Dare* in mid-story—left him, in fact, floating in the middle of the ocean in a Navy vessel. The last two panels of his last strip, which ran on December 1, 1934, show the villain Von Slugg. The submarine pirate and his men are in a cave on his private island. Von Slugg, hearing a strange sound, exclaims, "Vot's dot? I heard der sound uff un anchor chain rattling! Out mit der lights! It giffs trouble!" All Coulton Waugh had to do when he assumed command of the strip was figure out what was out there and what kind of trouble it was going to giff. Caniff, making the transition to *Terry* in somewhat of a hurry, had left behind no notes as to what happened next. Waugh, unlike most of the artists who inherited AP strips, had not come out of the bullpen. He'd never even met Caniff. Besides which, he had only a few days to come up with a week's sample strips. He took the few Caniff originals Wilson Hicks could locate around the office plus some proofs. He slept little and drank a lot of coffee, which finally resulted in his continuing the story without the apparent missing of a beat. "Dickie and Dan, aboard a Navy destroyer, have lured the pirate sub back to its island—At night the fighting gobs land from their boats," his first Monday strip began. On Tuesday Dickie, Dan, and Wags are charging uphill toward the pirates' stronghold.

The fact that Dickie was aboard a destroyer and the villain was down in a submarine when Caniff went away gave the strip a distinct marine flavor, which is probably the reason Waugh got the job. When he'd first called on Hicks to show his portfolio the gruff editor held up a thick stack of file cards and told him, "These are all the names of people I'd use before you." Waugh's father, however, was the noted marine painter Frederick Waugh. While Coulton Waugh wanted to be more than an imitator of his well-known father, he, too, was fascinated with the sea and sailing. The samples he showed the AP gave evidence of this. Somebody who knew how to draw boats and ships was going to have to pick up after Caniff. Hicks, apparently putting aside his deck of other possibilities, called Waugh in to try out for the task. "I'm not basically a figure man," Waugh told me. "But I loved boats, nature, the out-of-doors." Working very close to the Caniff style, Waugh did a daily and brought it in. All Hicks said about it was, "Try again." Waugh went back home, drank more coffee, and tried again. He began to feel more sure of himself. When Hicks saw the new samples he produced a contract, tossed it over to Waugh. It was for six months. Waugh would stay with *Dickie Dare*, off and on, until the 1950s.

He wrote and drew the strip, sticking fairly close in tone and style to what had gone before. For the first six months at least. As AP offered him contracts for longer and longer periods, Waugh came to feel the strip was his own and not Caniff's anymore. He swung away from the stiff, cartoony look, using brush lines for the figures and trying pen patterns—cross-hatching, graded lines, and the like—on the backgrounds. He finally arrived at what he felt was a "satisfying style." Waugh identified with the exuberant young

161

Dickie, and for most of the run of the feature he let him remain this side of his teens. "Keeping him twelve," he told me, "kept him safe from all the complexities of adolescence." He believed the important thing about Dickie was that he was a "kid trying to adjust to

DICKIE DARE   Boy Overboard

Coulton Waugh's love of the sea, its beauties and dangers, shows in these two 1938 Dickie Dare *dailies.* © *1938 AP. Reprinted by permission.*

the difficulties of the world with nothing but drive and energy. . . .
I'd been on my own from a very early age, too." While the seafaring
under Caniff had been only an interlude in a series of varied adventures, Coulton Waugh kept *Dickie Dare* a strip "based on the sea."
Almost every story had something to do with the sea, with ships

DICKIE DARE New Day—New World

and sailing. Waugh mingled his own fondness for sailing (Dickie had his own yawl, named the *Dickie Dare*) with ingredients from Robert Louis Stevenson, John Masefield, and other sea adventurers. There were episodes of sailing, episodes of diving for hidden treasure. Nature abounded; there were always plenty of birds and animals—from friendly chimps to vicious lions. Although Waugh's figure work improved (he got particularly good with villains, modeling them after his friends and assistants), it was always at ships and landscapes that he excelled. His *Dickie Dare*, from the late thirties and early forties, is a handsome strip.

Prior to going to work for AP, Waugh had done caricatures and spot drawings for the *New York World*. His reason for seeking a regular job was the need to finance his painting. Most of his friends and fellow artists told him that he couldn't do a strip during the week and paint on weekends. But he did. His paintings are in several museums, and during his lifetime he had several shows at New York galleries. He did a successful book, *How to Paint with a Knife*, for Watson-Guptill, and at the time of his death in May of 1973, was at work on another. In order to try a new strip for the newspaper *PM* and to write a history of comic strips, Waugh quit *Dickie* for several years in the mid-forties. The strip stayed in the family, though, since Odin Burvik, who carried it on, was his wife. *Hank*, a liberal adventure strip about a returning GI, lasted only a few months. After Waugh completed *The Comics*, the best general history so far, he took up *Dickie Dare* again. Between Odin and the return of Coulton Waugh, an undistinguished artist named Fran Matera had briefly drawn the strip. As the years passed, Waugh ceased to identify as closely with his boy hero. "After a long time I got a little bit fed up with Dickie and his 12-year-old reactions." He allowed Dickie, with the syndicate's approval, to mature a few years. Dickie became a naval cadet. When the Associated Press finally decided to let its strips die, *Dickie Dare* went with them. Waugh's last daily shows Dickie, appropriately, sailing away.

Chapter 9
Musclemen and Palookas

MOST OF THE adventure-strip leading men, and a few of the women, were pretty tough and handy with their dukes. This was usually, though, in addition to being daredevil pilots, deep-sea divers, or soldiers-of-fortune. But there were also funny-paper heroes whose major attribute was the ability to punch somebody in the nose. Some did it in the prize ring, while others saved their punches for archfiends and Martian invaders. The sports heroes had been celebrated in comic strips from the 1920s on, the superheroes were children of the late 1930s.

In the first two decades of this century, cartoonists were not thought of as too respectable, which may have been one reason why a lot of them liked to hang around with other semi-outcasts, such as actors and professional athletes. One of the first artists to exploit his lowlife connections was Tad Dorgan, whose widely circulated panel *Outdoor Sports* (it alternated with *Indoor Sports*) provided an insider's view of boxing, baseball, etc. *Mutt & Jeff*, of course, was even older and had originally been created to pass out horse-racing tips. Once it caught on and was syndicated, Bud Fisher and his various ghosts dropped the tips in favor of reworking vaudeville jokes. In the summer of 1922 Billy DeBeck, another celebrator of

American lowlife, was inspired to have his Barney Google fall heir to a racehorse named Spark Plug. This made a rich man of both Google and DeBeck, eventually even inspiring Billy Rose and a couple of his pals to write a song. While DeBeck used continuity, building suspense by stretching a race across a week or more, he was always a comedian determined to get a laugh in each strip. Less funny and somewhat closer to being an adventure strip was *You Know Me, Al.* Credited to Ring Lardner and based on his baseball stories about Jack Keefe, the strip was drawn by Tad's clumsy brother, Dick Dorgan. Not much of a strip, it managed to hang on for several years in the twenties. The first really successful straight sports strip was the creation of a pugnacious young man from Wilkes Barre. He was a mediocre writer and could barely draw, but he had an idea and he believed he could sell it.

Hammond Edward Fisher claims he had been nurturing the idea for almost a decade before it was accepted. Depending on which autobiographical piece you read, the inspiration hit him in either 1920 or 1921. "One day, while talking to an unsophisticated but good-natured prizefighter, I was suddenly hit by the idea for *Joe Palooka.* I rushed back to the office, wrote a continuity and made the first drawings of *Palooka.* Joe and I went immediately to New York, offered ourselves to all the syndicates, and were turned down by all of them. . . . We kept returning to New York, whenever we had the money. But nobody seemed to want *Joe Palooka.* . . . I went to New York in 1927 with two dollars and fifty cents over my carfare, landed a job in the advertising department of the *New York Daily News.* . . . Then I left the *News* and went to McNaught Syndicate and for the first time had the good fortune to meet Charles V. McAdam, general manager and vice-president, who offered to try out *Joe Palooka* the following year. I insisted upon going out and selling the strip to the newspapers myself. To prove my sales ability, I first took *Dixie Dugan,* which had been offered to all the newspapers before. Only two papers had bought the strip and the amount of revenue did not even pay for one day's engraving expenses." The forceful Fisher shoved the *Dixie* strip, then called *Show Girl,* into over two dozen papers. "Then I insisted on going out and selling Palooka. . . . While McAdam was on vacation in Florida, I took *Joe Palooka* on the road and sold the strip to twenty papers in three weeks." An insight into Ham Fisher's sales methods can be obtained from the autobiography of Emile Gauvreau, headman on Bernarr Macfadden's *Graphic* before becoming editor of the *Daily*

Mirror. "I bought my last comic strip one New Year's eve when Ham Fisher, known in New York circles as the 'pride of Wilkes-Barre, Pa.,' an enthusiastic cartoonist who sought to introduce his wares to the metropolis, befuddled me with a rare bottle of Burgundy during a hilarious celebration. When I woke the next day I found I was sponsor of 'Joe Palooka,' an exemplary character who never drank or smoked and was good to his mother. Strangely enough 'Palooka' became one of the most successful ventures in the comic field and soon had Fisher living in affluence and riding an Arabian horse in Central Park."

Fisher's achievement in selling his strip, even with the aid of liquor, was considerable. *Joe Palooka* in 1930 was a most ungodly looking thing. Though Fisher later claimed he was years ahead of everybody else in inventing a straight continuity strip, the first *Palooka* dailies were drawn in a very shaky imitation of the other Fisher's *Mutt & Jeff.* Rumors persist, at least among older cartoonists, that Ham Fisher never even drew the sample weeks of *Joe Palooka* but hired a high school art student to whip them up for him. Lyman Anderson told me he can remember being stopped on a Manhattan street by Fisher in the late 1920s and offered a chance to illustrate a great strip idea. Anderson turned him down.

The early Joe Palooka was pretty much of a rube, and early continuities were built around his dumbness. He wins the heavyweight title in 1931 by a fluke. This victory had a pronounced effect on him and his manager, Knobby Walsh, an ex-haberdasher. They both become much better looking, Joe's hair turns from black to blond. His stupidity begins to recede, though he never ceases saying, "youse." The reason for these improvements in everybody's looks is that Ham Fisher was not well off enough to hire better ghosts. The list of twenty subscribing papers had grown to several hundred. Ann Howe, Joe's society-girl sweetheart, made her first appearance in 1932. The earlier artist, whether Fisher himself or that high school boy, could never have drawn a pretty blonde like her. The following year Fisher signed on his best-known assistant, setting the stage for a bitter feud which would continue throughout his lifetime. Like most oft-told tales, there are several versions of how Ham Fisher first met Al Capp. The most sentimental version, most nearly akin to the softhearted continuities of the *Palooka* pages, appeared in Martin Sheridan's *Comics and Their Creators* in 1942:

"Al returned to art school in Massachusetts and landed in New York in 1933 with six dollars. While walking along the street near

Central Park South, a long car of expensive make pulled up beside him.

"'I've made a bet with my sister that the roll under your arm consists of cartoons,' the driver said.

"'You're right,' Al smiled.

"The man in the car introduced himself as Ham Fisher, the cartoonist of *Joe Palooka,* and offered Al a job as assistant."

Capp already had visions of hillbillies dancing in his head, so it was only natural he'd introduce them into the *Palooka* saga. While barnstorming through the South, Joe is matched against the Tennessee hill champ Big Leviticus. A year later Capp left his mentor to set up in his own hillbilly business with *Li'l Abner.* As late as 1942 he was speaking kindly of Fisher: "I owe most of my success to him, for I learned many tricks of the trade while working alongside of him." There was some cooling, and in 1948 Fisher was openly accusing Capp of stealing his ideas. Capp's remembrance of that incident near the park had changed. *Newsweek* reported, "In 1933 Fisher literally picked him off the street. Capp insists Fisher thought he was a syndicate messenger, but the latter claims he recognized Al as a hapless young cartoonist ('I was a literate gentleman, and Mr. Capp a wild-haired boy')." When Fisher brought Leviticus back into his strip, he bluntly announced to his readers, "The first hillbillies ever to appear in a comic strip were Big Leviticus and his family. Any resemblance to our original hillbillies is certainly not a coincidence." This prompted Capp to complain to the National Cartoonists Society that Fisher was "reflecting discredit on the society." As to their personal relationship, Capp told *Newsweek,* "I tried to ignore him. I regard him like a leper. I feel sorry for him but I shun him."

Ham Fisher's feelings toward Capp did not mellow with the passage of the years. Unlike Palooka, he was not much for forgiving. He is said to have later carried on a campaign among fellow cartoonists to prove that *Li'l Abner* was pornographic. He carried wads of clipped Capp strips around with him, along with the ever-present long lists of all the papers currently carrying *Joe Palooka.* Capp struck back in that magazine for literate gentlemen, the *Atlantic Monthly.* The April 1950 issue contained his "I Remember Monster," several thousand anti-Fisher words. Though never mentioning him by name, Capp made it quite clear who he meant.

"When fans ask me, 'How does a normal-looking fella like you think up all those—*b-r-r!!!*—creatures?' I always evade a straightforward answer. Because the truth is I don't think'em up. I was lucky enough to know them—all of them—and what was even luckier, all in the person of one man. One veritable gold mine of swinishness. It was my privilege, as a boy, to be associated with a certain treasure trove of lousiness, who, in the normal course of each day of his life, managed to be, in dazzling succession, every conceivable kind of heel."

From the perspective of his own affluence, Capp's depression job with Fisher didn't look so good. "He paid me $22 a week, and although I had no responsibilities but just one wife, one baby, one cellar apartment, and only one kid brother at Ohio State who needed $3 a week to live on (he lived on carrots and unguarded milk), I wasn't a good manager I guess. I was always broke near the end of the week." Capp finished off his piece with, "The wounded have been beguiled by books and sermons and comic strips into believing that something called Life Itself will, itself, punish Evil. Mostly, it doesn't. It didn't punish my Benefactor. He grew richer and healthier, more famous and more honored. He kept no old friends, but he made lots of shiny new friends. Nothing happened. He just grew older and eviler."

Ham Fisher had no trouble hiring new assistants. The two men who worked with him longest were Phil Boyle and Moe Leff. Leff, and this is probably not a coincidence, had also been an assistant to Al Capp. The tremendous jump in quality which *Li'l Abner* made from the mid-thirties on, particularly with the addition of all those voluptuous women, was chiefly due to Leff. He'd drawn a Sunday page for United Features before joining Capp, a handsomely done kid-fantasy page titled *Peter Pat*. Moe Leff greatly improved the looks of the *Palooka* strip too, moving Joe even further from the rube image. He also drew the self-portrait of Ham Fisher that accompanies the *Comics and Their Creators* profile. Fisher probably had something to do with the writing of the feature, since Knobby's adventures seem to reflect some of Fisher's apparent feelings about himself. When Joe wasn't defending his title or hiding out from the law for a crime he didn't commit or serving in the French Foreign Legion, the strip concentrated on detailing Knobby's numerous unsuccessful romances.

Joe Palooka has frequently been held up as the liberal answer to *Little Orphan Annie*. Fisher's supposed liberalism, and his much-photographed relationships with FDR and Harry Truman, may have been real. But the *Palooka* strips plugging enlisting, several months before Pearl Harbor, and support for sundry other worthwhile liberal causes, read now like the most shallow kind of sound-truck rhetoric. "The freedom train as I said is being sent to over 300 of America's largest cities and it will give every man, woman, and child a chance to see the most thrilling documents in our history," Joe tells his handler in a typical fervid moment. "It will be guarded by U.S. Marines because aboard will be the Declaration of Independence. . . " When Joe finishes listing the contents of the train, the handler exclaims, "Say, Joe, what day will it be here? I want my kids to see it. I'd rather they'd see those than anything in the world!"

In spite of his success and friendships with celebrities (frequently mentioned in the strip), Fisher seems to have been an unhappy and unliked man. In a 1948 autobiographical strip, which *Collier's* magazine ran as part of a series on top cartoonists, Fisher is shown talking to an aspiring young cartoonist in the final panel. "It must be WONDERFUL. I'm gonna be a CARTOONIST, too," blurts the freckled youth. Fisher tells him, "PHOOEY! Lissen . . . ya doin' anything for dinner tonite . . . I'm LONESOME!" In 1955 he killed himself. Joe is still in the newspapers, though not in as many as during Fisher's day. The strip is drawn by the uninspired pen of Tony DiPreta. Joe is not a rube at all anymore, and he rarely fights.

Several sports strips came into being in the 1930s. Of varying degrees of seriousness, few of them survived the decade—*Rube Appleberry, Buck Haney, Bullet Benton, Ned Brant, Curly Harper*. Those last two were about college athletics. Ned's rather dull adventures were allegedly written by Bob Zupke, head football coach at the University of Illinois. Curly thrived only in a Sunday page which accompanied *Tim Tyler's Luck*. Credited to Lyman Young, the page was actually created and drawn by Nat Edson. A more successful jock-oriented feature was *Joe Jinks*. Joe had been in the funnies since 1918, starting life in *Joe's Car*, a strip drawn originally by Vic Forsythe for the *New York World*. Throughout the twenties Joe Jinks toyed with cars, then planes and various outdoor sports. A common strip type, Coulton Waugh described him as reflecting "a specific yearning in the souls of millions of men who resemble him closely . . . the nervous, exasperated little business husband. Physically stunted, with tiny chest and shoulders and sagging stomach, he has the usual out-reaching comic nose, scratchy mustache and pop eyes. His hair is falling out, and even when asleep, there is an exasperated set to the lines about his mouth and forehead which reflects the exhaustion brought on by the complex problem of earning money."

In the early thirties, after the strip had changed its name to *Joe Jinks*, he became a fight manager. In the comics—it occasionally even happens in real life—there can be more than one heavyweight champion of the world. Joe's fighter, Dynamite Dunn, held the heavyweight crown during most of the years when Joe Palooka was also heavyweight champ. Dynamite was a square-jawed fellow, in the Captain Easy mold, and a lot brighter than the other champ. Forsythe drew the strip until the thirties, then went over to Hearst to try similar things. He came back to Joe for a while before quitting for good. In *The Business of Cartooning*, published in 1939, Chuck Thorndike says, "The writer recently heard from Forsythe to the effect that he had a nervous crackup and had given up comic drawing and was devoting all his time to painting at San Marino, California."

Joe Jinks surely must hold the record for strips drawn by the most different artists. Pete Llanuza, sports cartoonist for the *World-Telegram*, did it until 1936. The Sunday page was then taken over by Moe Leff, with a little help from his brother Sam. After the Leffs left, Henry Formhals, who'd been ghosting the *Ella Cinders* Sunday and was now ghosting the *Freckles* dailies, assumed the Sunday. The daily, meantime, enjoyed a different batch of cartoonists. Harry Homan, political cartoonist and creator of a Sunday page called *Billy Make Believe*, handled the daily until his death in 1939. Then the *Joe Jinks* pen was passed from George Storm to Al Kostuk to Morris Weiss to Al Leiderman and finally to Sam Leff. Leff, working in a style which was a simplified version of his brother's, introduced Joe to a new prizefighter. This was Curly Kayoe. Joe became Curly's manager, Curly became heavyweight champ, and the strip changed its name to his.

In 1938 Jerry Siegel of Cleveland, Ohio, at long last managed to sell *Superman*. Like Ham Fisher, Siegel'd been struggling for years to get somebody to buy his idea, which was an amalgam of mythology, science fiction, Philip Wylie's novel *Gladiator,* and the pulp hero Doc Savage. Before teaming up with fellow SF fan Joe Shuster, Siegel had offered the job of drawing *Superman* to any artist who'd listen. Mel Graff, who'd started out in Cleveland, was among those approached by Siegel, but since there was no money involved he declined. M. C. Gaines, affiliated with the McClure Syndicate at the time, sent the sample strips over to the DC Comics offices when the first issue of *Action Comics* was being made up in 1938. *Superman*

171

Making his opponent see stars is Dynamite Dunn, one of the several heavyweight champs who practiced in the funnies. This particular Joe Jinks *daily was ghosted by the ubiquitous George Storm.* © 1940 United Features Syndicate, Inc. Reprinted by permission.

was accepted, Siegel and Shuster signed a contract which would eventually cause them to be screwed out of several million dollars each, and the age of the superhero began.

Comic books prospered beyond the wildest dreams of the handful of thick-witted schlock publishers who now found themselves in control of a fantastically profitable business. The syndicates became interested in superpeople and comic books in general. McClure, thanks to Gaines, got to distribute the *Superman* newspaper strip.

This began in 1939, a daily at first, joined by a Sunday page later in the year. Siegel and Shuster, still based in Cleveland, had long since hired a staff of artists to help them cope with the demand for more and more *Superman* material. They now employed Wayne Boring (he'd been in Toledo assisting on *Big Chief Wahoo*), Paul Cassidy, Dennis Neville, and others. Some of these men could approximate Shuster's style, inspired by Roy Crane's work, and some couldn't. It didn't seem to matter. As long as that guy in the trick suit was outrunning streamliners, leaping over tall buildings at a single bound, and saving the accident-prone Lois Lane, anybody could draw him and the sales would keep right on climbing.

All sorts of publishers got into comic books once the sales figures on *Action* and *Superman* became known. Large outfits and hole-in-the-wall operations, for a time they all prospered. One of the most vocal of the new publishers was a man named Victor S. Fox, whose Fox Feature Syndicate was responsible for *Wonderworld Comics, Mystery Men,* and *Fantastic*. While Fox took credit for inventing all the characters and magazines, all the work in his titles was sweatshop produced, most of it by the Eisner-Iger boys. Fox had the ear of *Editor & Publisher,* where his pronouncements on the future of newspaper strips appeared under headlines like "Fox Sees Adventure Comics in Ascendancy" and "Format Change Won't Help Comics, Says Fox." It was Fox's theory that what everybody wanted now was the type of "thriller" material which only comic books, particularly those of the Fox line, could deliver. All this was prelude to his offering comic strips of his own. Fox had available daily-strip versions of his comic-book heroes, as well as a four-page readyprint Sunday section. He later added a sixteen-page comic-book section as well. The daily strips included *The Green Mask, Spark Stevens,* and *The Blue Beetle.* Jack Kirby did the *Beetle* daily for a while, as did the champion Fox hack, Louis Cazeneuve. The readyprint supplement was made up of recycled comic-book art squeezed into Sunday-page shape. Lou Fine's *Flame* and Dick Briefer's *Rex Dexter of Mars* were among the features thus mangled. Having never seen a copy of the sixteen-page comic-book section, I can't say for sure if it ever existed anywhere but in the boasts of Victor Fox.

Even the substantial *Chicago Tribune* was frightened by the rise of the funny book. In the spring of 1940 it introduced a supplement of its own, named forthrightly *Comic Book Magazine.* Apparently nobody up in the Tower knew what a comic book was. Early issues

173

contained a revived *Texas Slim* by Ferd Johnson, along with reprints of Gaar Williams's *Mort Green & Wife* and Frank King's *Bobby Make-Believe* (not to be confused with Homan's *Billy*). The rest of the pages ran the toppers of current *Trib* Sunday pages—*Corky, Josie,* and so forth. Not the stuff of which thrillers are made, as Victor Fox could have told them. Soon, however, some of the Chicago-based cartoonists began to do original strips for the *Comic Book*. George Merkle, who'd done some funny-book work, came up with *Hy Score* ("his name is Henry Score but nicknamed by friends 'Hy' for short"). Hy was a secret agent for Army intelligence, Merkle wasn't much of an artist. C. C. Cooper drew *Fighting with Daniel Boone*. Ed Moore did the only newspaper strip he ever got to sign, *Captain Storm*. Jack Ryan drew *Streamer Kelly,* about a heroic fireman. Bert Whitman batted out *Mr. Ex*. Besides competing with real comic books, the *Comic Book* was a tryout ground for new features. The only real success to come out of it was Dale Messick's *Brenda Starr,* which began there on June 30,1940.

"Everyone had left for the day at the Eisner & Iger Studio and the office was silent . . . like a tomb, I thought. Only a few days ago Busy Arnold and I closed a deal. He and Henry Martin had lined up a handful of papers—enough to start on. There was a 'however,' however. I had to sell my interest in Eisner & Iger and devote myself fully to a new venture—a Sunday comic supplement to be syndicated nationally. It would be 16 pages containing 3 features . . . I would write the lead and create the other two. A full-time job indeed. The problem now really was: create the feature." This is Will Eisner, his sense of the dramatic functioning as usual, remembering what it was like in the spring of 1940, when he was twenty-three and on the brink of creating *The Spirit*. Eisner had by then been in the comic-book business longer than almost anybody. His first work had appeared in 1936 in a short-lived magazine called *Wow*. Forming a partnership with Jerry Iger, *Wow*'s editor and a former Hearst cartoonist, Eisner opened one of the first comic-book sweatshops. "I was running a shop in which we made comic book features pretty much the way Ford made cars. . . . We made $1.50 a page net profit. I got very rich before I was 22." Among the early drudges in the shop were Bob Kane, Dick Briefer, Mort Meskin, Bob Powell, and Lou Fine. Eventually they mass-produced art for the Quality and Fiction House lines of comics as well as for the aforementioned Victor Fox. Eisner also experimented with several features which could swing both ways and be either newspaper strips or comic-book pages. One of the

Ed Moore's Captain Storm, *one of the sample pages that got him a berth with the* Chicago Tribune's Comic Book Magazine.

Eisner-Iger clients was the Editors Press Service, which translated American strips for Latin American markets and also produced a weekly English-language tabloid of strips for distribution in Australia and England. Called *Wags*, and priced at tuppence, the tab offered *Tarzan, Dick Tracy, Terry, Tailspin Tommy,* and others, plus several pages original with it. These included *Hawks of the Sea,* conceived and mostly drawn by Eisner, *Sheena* by Meskin, and *Peter Pupp,* a *Mickey Mouse* sort of thing by Bob Kane. After running in the antipodes, these pages were reprinted in this country in *Jumbo Comics,* with *Hawks* also showing up in *Feature Funnies.*

Feature was owned in part by the Register & Tribune Syndicate. After Eisner and Everett "Busy" Arnold had come up with the idea of a sixteen-page comic-book insert, Arnold, who ran *Feature* and the rest of the Quality line, sold it to Henry Martin of the R&T Syndicate. Arnold had already tried out a sample insert on some newspaper editors. According to Steranko, in his history of the comic books, "Arnold showed some of George Brenner's old work on *The Clock.* Neubold of the *Washington Star* liked the idea, but not the artist. He selected another strip, one by Lou Fine. Arnold knew Fine couldn't handle the writing end of a weekly strip and might even be too slow to meet the art deadlines. But he knew who could do both. "That's Bill Eisner's work," he volunteered. Things like that happened to Lou Fine for the rest of his life. Apparently the Register & Tribune was more enthusiastic about the idea of a comic-book insert than about *The Spirit.* The initial announcement in the trades quoted the syndicate's Martin as saying the book would offer "three complete features in each issue with the same characters appearing in new episodes weekly. The material is all original." No mention of Eisner or his characters.

Let's get back to Eisner in that tomblike studio in the spring of 1940. "The hero would have to be someone who could operate unfettered by the rules—so he could go anywhere and do anything I would want him to do. Dolan, the cop, would be the establishment, and Ellen, the daughter would be the love interest. By midnight of that night I had all the 7 pages roughly laid out and I was ready to write copy, flesh out the plot. . . . [Arnold] was a little disappointed. This was the age of costumed characters—when was I going to put the Spirit in a costume? Some newspaper customers suggested it. I said I'd think about it. . . . I compromised. I put a mask on the Spirit." Actually, in his first Sunday-supplement appearance the Spirit forgot to wear his mask. He didn't show up in that until the second week.

Will Eisner was a great reader of short stories, and an enthusiastic movie fan. He began trying to imitate his favorite writers, O. Henry and Ambrose Bierce, while fooling increasingly with motion-picture-camera approaches to layout. The radio must have had an influence on him as well, since he came to use sound effects and narration in the *Spirit* stories. Eisner had a sense of humor, meaning he never took his hero seriously. "I could never understand why any crimefighter would go out and fight crime. Why the hell a guy should run around with a mask and fight crime was beyond me. Except that I, and there again it was a part of my background, this kind of mystical thinking, in which I've always felt that people do the things they have to do. . . . You put a man in front of a wall, he will climb that wall. As he builds a society, he builds a wall and then struggles to climb it. The Spirit had all the middle class motivations, which is that 'I've got to have something to do. This is my thing, this is my schtick.' Of course, the big thing, the big problem each week was to figure out an acceptable reason why he should get involved in this in the first place." In his stories Eisner used supervillains, sultry sirens, and the other essentials of comic books, but he also took an interest in more earthy things. Civic corruption, life on the underside of a large city, all were topics for *Spirit* adventures. Even when muck-raking Eisner was not completely serious, his approach was akin to that of Preston Sturges in a film like *The Great McGinty*. The artwork and the story lines made the *Spirit* Sunday section the only one of the batch of comic-book-inspired supplements to survive. In October of 1941 a daily strip was added. Eisner had a number of artists working on the *Spirit*, in whole or part: Alex Kotzky, Lou Fine, Gill Fox, Klaus Nordling, John Spranger, and Jack Cole. Cole, one of the most inventive cartoonists in comic books and the creator of another hero with a sense of humor, *Plastic Man*, soloed on several daily sequences. The strip lasted only a few years, but the booklet continued until 1952. Because Eisner was a bit shrewder than many of his contemporaries, he owns *The Spirit* and the income from current reprints is his.

About the only superhero to start from scratch in the newspapers was the Red Knight. The Knight, debuting in mid-1940, was not a comic-book retread, nor were his creators funny-book vets. They were John J. Welch and Jack W. McGuire, who'd been collaborating off and on throughout the thirties on *Slim & Tubby* and its various transmutations. McGuire's drawing, forceful and possessed of a sloppy charm, could have fit into the eclectic comic-book field of the

A Spirit *daily from 1942, fittingly a ghosted one. The artist, in case you can't tell, is Jack Cole.* © 1975 Will Eisner. Reprinted by permission.

time. He was one of the busiest cartoonists around. Besides doing his six *Red Knight* dailies, he taught art in a Texas high school and ghosted six *Ella Cinders* dailies and a Sunday every week. Like his comic-book peers, the Knight had a secret origin. "In his secret laboratory, secluded deep in a wood, Dr. Van Lear is completing an incredible experiment that is destined to astound the whole world," explains Welch's first caption. Dr. Van Lear adds, "Finished! My scientific masterpiece! A man who through chemical process will become all powerful in body and mind! He shall be the Red Knight!" After charging the Knight up with Plus Power, the doctor tells him,

THE RED KNIGHT--

Des Moines's answer to the Superman *craze was* The Red Knight. *The Knight wasn't too bright, even for a superhero.* © 1941 Register & Tribune Syndicate. Reprinted by permission.

"There is much good you can do in this troubled world!" He can perform all sorts of superhero stuff, even turn invisible, but there is a hitch. "Your weakness is that the 'Plus Power' wears off—You must return frequently to be revitalized." The Knight turned out to have one other weakness—the public didn't take to him. The strip ended abruptly in 1943.

Closer to being a true comic-book-type feature was Tarpe Mills's *Miss Fury*. A Sunday page, originally titled *Black Fury*, it started on April 6, 1941. Miss Mills had been laboring in comic books since the late thirties, responsible for things like *Daredevil Barry Finn, Fantastic Films, Mann of India,* and, one of my favorite titles, *The Purple Zombie*. Of the few women then drawing for comic books, Tarpe Mills was the only one, excuse the sexist remark, with a masculine style. Not only masculine, but hardboiled. Her Sunday page was full of action and grandstanding violence. In her first month of Sundays, Miss Fury, after surviving an auto crash, claws a detective across the face, steps on his gun hand, kicks him in the face, and then sees to it that a heavy almost goes through the windshield of a car. She did not have any superpowers. By day she was lovely socialite Marla Drake, by night she slipped into a black leopard-skin to fight crime. Tarpe Mills also seems to have been influenced by some under-the-counter literature. There are quite a few of the traditional bondage elements in the feature—whips, branding irons, spike-heel shoes, men beating women, women tearing each other's clothes off, and a handsome selection of frilly lingerie.

A few mystery men from other media had a brief go-round as newspaper heroes at about this time. The Shadow, invisible on radio and visible in the pulps, was featured in a daily strip by Vernon Greene and Walter Gibson. In writing the strip, Gibson—under the alias Maxwell Grant he produced almost all the *Shadow* pulp novels—used the radio show as a model. The funny-paper Shadow was in reality wealthy man-about-town Lamont Cranston, and he had the ability, picked up years ago in the Orient, to cloud men's minds so they couldn't see him. Distributed by Gibson's onetime employers, the Philadelphia Ledger Syndicate, the *Shadow* comic strip never did well. When a comic book was started in 1940, Gibson had Vern Greene cut up the daily originals to make comic-book pages out of them.

Even less of a hit was the *Green Hornet* comic strip. "I obtained rights to the Green Hornet radio feature through luck and salesmanship," Bert Whitman recalls. "It started me off on a publishing

Something for everybody in Tarpe Mills's Miss Fury *(Originally known as* Black Fury*). © 1941 Bell Syndicate, Inc. Reprinted by permission.*

venture. I found someone who wanted to invest in my know-how and I was off to a flying start. I had complete rights to the Green Hornet for newspapers and comic books." Whitman may have had know-how, he wasn't much of a cartoonist. He got help in handling the *Hornet*. Irwin Hasen, Hal Sharp, and others did the comic book; Frank Robbins penciled the newspaper strip. This was during the same period Robbins was writing and drawing *Scorchy Smith* for AP. Although the public was fond of the adventures of Britt Reid, Kato, and Axford on the radio three nights a week, they weren't interested in looking at them every day in the newspaper. After the war, when Whitman had long since sold out to the Harvey comics organization, there was talk of having another try at doing a *Hornet* strip. Bill Finger, co-inventor of *Batman*, was to write it, with overseeing by Frank Striker. Bob Powell, then doing the *Shadow* comic books and numerous features for Harvey, was first in line to do the drawing. The project never got beyond the conference stage.

Chapter 10
You Betchum!

So STURDY A hero is the cowboy that he can thrive almost anywhere. He has galloped across movie screens since the century began, in Westerns filmed everywhere from New Jersey to Tokyo. He's jingled his spurs through tons of novels, shot it out with owlhoots on the rough pages of innumerable pulp magazines. There's never been a television season without at least one cowboy. And before that there were cowboys, their fiery horses' hoofbeats produced by chest-thumping sound men, spilling out of the radio at all hours. Cowboys, not surprisingly, also turned up on the comic pages. A few landed during the first big wave of adventure strips in the twenties, a larger batch arrived in the thirties deluge.

In his *Minute Movies* Ed Wheelan had been using cowboy continuities from the early 1920s, in such serials as *Desert Danger, Way Out West,* and *The Great Open Spaces.* By the late 1920s there were several full-time Wild West strips. Among the early arrivals was a lad known, eventually, as Broncho Bill. He was no relation to Broncho Billy of the silents, and he's done business under a couple of other names before settling on that one. Harry O'Neill's strip, one of the first offered by United Features, came into the world as *Young Buffalo Bill.* By the early thirties it was *Buckaroo Bill,* changing to

Broncho Bill for its final decade or so. A graduate of the Landon mail-order cartoon school, O'Neill is one of the few professional acrobats ever to draw a comic strip. The stories in *Broncho Bill* came to center around the activities of a Bill-led group of youthful vigilantes calling themselves the Rangers, sort of gun-toting boy scouts. O'Neill's idea of suspense was to have some innocent, a hapless infant or a golden-haired little girl, about to fall over a cliff or be eaten by a grizzly bear. He inked in a flowery Old World style that didn't quite hide the strange, out-of-kilter drawing beneath it. O'Neill marched to a different drummer, one with one leg shorter than the other. His writing matched his artwork: "They go for their guns but Bill clutches at an empty holster. In his haste he had forgotten to rearm," for instance, or "Bill's gesture of friendship to Bull Redmond didn't alter this scoundrel's determination to raid the Circle B herd. Bull now is preparing to start the forest fire that he hopes will distract the young rancher's attention."

A cowboy feature which began as a half-serious continuity strip and later switched to the gag-a-day format was *Mescal Ike*. "In the late twenties S. L. Huntley and I got together and started *Mescal Ike*," cartoonist Art Huhta recalled recently. "The *Chicago Daily News* had launched a syndicate and we were lucky, they took us on. The syndicate lasted about three years and folded. We got offers from both Bell and United Features. We chose Bell. . . . Huntley worked in an ad agency writing copy, later he wrote soap opera for radio. . . . We did our *Mescal Ike* ideas over the telephone and between horse races. He liked the races. At times I wound up doing the ideas as well as the art." Always drawn in a cartoon style, the strip went in for the continued-tomorrow approach in its early years. White-hatted Mescal was the hero, his shaggy partner was named Dirty Shirt Mulloney, and cantankerous, bewhiskered Pa Piffle was another regular. The adventures took place in and around the southwestern desert town of Cactus Center. The action was built around searches for lost mine deeds, run-ins with bandits, and the sundry other conventions of Western melodrama. There was also considerable joke-cracking. By the early 1930s only the jokes remained. The strip lasted until 1940. For most of the years he drew it, Huhta shared a Chicago studio with Sol Hess and Wally Carlson of *The Nebbs*, and also lent a hand on their strip.

Just as there were aviation comic strips drawn by men who'd actually piloted planes, there were cowpoke strips by artists who'd actually been up on a horse. Fred Harman was one such, having grown up on his dad's ranch in Colorado. After a brief spell in the National Guard during World War I, Harman went back to the cowpuncher's life. In the middle twenties he wandered to Kansas City and got into newspaper work as an artist. He and his brother, Hugh, got interested in the burgeoning art of animation, and for a time Fred Harman was in partnership with Kansas City's other cartoonist, Walt Disney. But when Walt moved out to Hollywood, Harman didn't follow. He did go there a few years later, after having acquired a wife and a son. Determined to become the Will James of the funny papers, Harman created, in the early thirties, a cowboy strip called *Bronc Peeler*. He used to "travel up and down the West

BRONC PEELER Close Call for Pete By FRED HARMAN

Early Bronc Peeler, before he acquired Little Beaver and broad shoulders.

185

Coast in a car, drawing and selling his strip at the same time." Fred Harman Features, as he called himself, also peddled *Bosko,* which was based on the animated-cartoon character concocted by Hugh Harman and Rudolf Ising. Bronc, who hung around with a mustached galoot name of Coyote Pete, was a gangling red-headed youth. As the strip progressed, Harman, a redhead himself, added a few years to Bronc's age and some inches to his shoulders, making him less of a mooncalf. In the Sunday page, still under the spell of Will James, Harman gave his readers not only twelve panels of Western adventure but a scenic view of the West as well. The panel, titled *On the Range,* ran underneath the Peeler half-page and was always accompanied by a few paragraphs of Harman's best aw-shucks prose: "History books tell us about wild Injuns an' how they killed white people. When they weren't killin' cowboys an' soldiers, they were fightin' other Injun tribes. But shucks, ya can't blame them fer all the massacres. They were pikers compared to us folks"; "Did ya ever come face to face with yerself at a waterin' hole? No foolin' it'll give ya thoughts ya never stopped to think about—A feelin' of humbleness . . . "

Bronc Peeler was a hard-riding, fast-shooting hombre, good with his fists and attractive to the ladies. He dropped final *g*s as often as he could, called his horse a hoss, and referred to Coyote Pete as m'pal. Harman drew in a gruff, forceful style, having no fears about his ability to depict the horses, cattle, and other cowboy objects that often defeated dude cartoonists. His stories, though, came not out of the West but from the pages of the pulps and off the movie screens. Bronc dealt with rustlers, Mexican bandits, crooked lawyers, and tinhorn gamblers. At the suggestion of his wife, Harman gave Bronc a boy sidekick in hopes of winning a larger juvenile audience. The kid was an Indian named Little Beaver (after his late father Chief Beaver). For a man who professed to love Injuns, Harman made Little Beaver the worst kind of Uncle Tomming Hollywood Indian. His clothes, Harman admitted, were not authentic. And his conversation was a triumph of Poverty Row patois: "Me sneakum away to trailum . . . Don't tellum nobody!" About this time Fred Harman's work came to the notice of New York entrepreneur Stephen Slesinger. Slesinger was an agent, merchandiser, and promoter. He controlled, for instance, all United States merchandising rights to *Winnie the Pooh.* He was also into comic-book publishing and the production of comic strips. Inviting Harman East, Slesinger had him convert Bronc into Red Ryder. Little Beaver remained Little Beaver ("You betchum!") and became Red's constant companion.

Stephen Slesinger, Inc., sold the renamed cowboy to NEA in 1938 and subsequently promoted *Red Ryder* movie serials (starring Don "Red" Barry), B-movies, comic books, novels, and a radio show ("From out of the West comes America's famous fighting cowboy—Red Ryder!"). Red also supplanted earlier cowboys as spokesman for the Daisy Manufacturing Company, and throughout the 1940s he hawked BB guns on the back covers of comic books. Little Beaver helped out too: "You gettum carbine like Red Ryder's heap soon!" Harman appeared in the ads along with his characters. "Fred Harman, famous cowboy artist who draws the popular NEA newspaper cartoon RED RYDER COMIC STRIP was a sure 'nough Colorado cowboy before hittin' the trail to New York City. Fred helped Daisy design this genuine Western-style saddle carbine an' hopes you get your RED RYDER CARBINE right away!" By now Harman had settled on his Red Ryder Rancho near Pagosa Springs, Colorado. Daisy ran several contests which offered as first prize "2 FREE TRIPS to the ranch" where you could "SEE Fred Harman DRAW his famous Cartoon Strip." Slesinger, never missing a bet, was active in the Boys Clubs of America, and he saw to it that the winner of the organization's Boy of the Year contest always won a trip to the rancho.

Publicity releases and interviews always stressed the fact that Harman was a compulsive artist who loved nothing better than drawing.

"Some days Harman takes his sketch pad, mounts his horse and rides out to sketch herds in the surrounding countryside. Drawing cattle, Indians and Mexicans is his great passion. . . . He uses these sketches to develop his Sunday page.

"He has no assistants, which among strip cartoonists is unusual. He is a perfectionist temperamentally incapable of working with a helper. An assistant might not know the difference between a California, single or center-file rig and that, of course, would be calamitous."

Actually *Red Ryder* was written and drawn by divers hands. Some of the ghost artists, like Jim Gary, worked out of the Slesinger office in the East. Others, like John Wade Hampton and Edmond Good, actually spent time at the famous rancho.

After he had been with NEA for many years, Harman switched to the McNaught Syndicate. When Stephen Slesinger died in the early 1950s, most of the subsidiary uses of the *Red Ryder* property had ended. The strip itself hung on a few more years. During its last days Harman deserted his cowboy, possibly to devote full time to his paintings, and the strip was credited to Bob MacLeod.

An even more marketable cowboy was the Lone Ranger. He was the joint creation of a Detroit radio-station owner and a Buffalo pulp writer. George W. Trendle, who owned station WXYZ, wanted to compete with the networks. He decided to do it with a show about a cowboy with Robin Hood and Zorro tendencies. He hired Frank Striker to write the scripts. The half-hour show, heard three times a week, went on the air in January of 1933. Success was immediate; the masked man was soon heard all across the country, sponsored by seventeen different bread companies. Before he'd even moved onto the network, Trendle offered a free pop gun to the first three hundred kids who wrote in. That offer pulled 25,904 responses. By 1940 a Lone Ranger premium offer would draw letters from a million listeners. Realizing that here was a property to reckon with, Trendle formed the Lone Ranger, Inc., and merchandised like crazy. There were Lone Ranger guns, Lone Ranger costumes, Lone Ranger books, *Lone Ranger* movie serials, and, from the fall of 1938 onward, a *Lone Ranger* comic strip.

The earliest *Lone Ranger* releases, both daily and Sunday, were credited to Frank Striker and artist Ed Kressy. Kressy, who worked in a somewhat cartoony style, had trouble getting the masked man's eyes to look right behind the mask. Sometimes the pupils would be little black dots, sometimes tiny circles with a dot in the middle. No matter what Kressy tried, the Lone Ranger's eyes always looked funny. There must have been other dissatisfactions with Kressy's weak-looking Lone Ranger and bland Tonto very soon after the strip commenced. His name was left on for the rest of the year, but other men were obviously doing the drawing. The best of these temporaries was Jon Blummer, who had a more forceful style. He began working in comic books a year later, when he created *Hop Harrigan*. For some reason Blummer wasn't kept on. When he left, in early 1939, King Features, distributors of the strip, turned to the bullpen and old reliable Charles Flanders. Flanders was still doing, as best he could, his Alex Raymond act. The Lone Ranger became immediately more virile-seeming, better matching the impression conveyed by the radio voice. Although Flanders's mask covered most of the Ranger's nose, he didn't have any trouble with the eyes. The stories in the comic strip were pretty much like those of the radio show, with more pretty girls in sight. Tonto gave the impression he'd studied English at the same reservation school as Little Beaver: "Me hearum talk with Barton! You try killum Lone Ranger!"

Charles Flanders peaked on the *Lone Ranger* in the middle 1940s. From then on, in part due to personal problems, his work steadily declined. He took to drawing everybody from the back, to save himself the trouble of having to worry about faces, and always cut a figure off as high up as he could. Whole Sunday pages toward the end seem to consist of nothing but the backs of heads and a few scraggly trees in the distance. There were periods when he was apparently unable to do the feature at all. Tom Gill, responsible for the comic-book version of the Lone Ranger's adventures, usually filled in. The strip, growing ever more feeble, managed to reach the 1970s before breathing its last.

Zane Grey, of Zanesville, Ohio, gave up his dental practice in 1904 to follow what he thought of as a literary career. By 1915 his woodenly written, but action-packed, Western adventure novels were hitting the bestseller lists. Throughout the 1920s Grey's clumsy works were continually on the lists, often at the very top. "After a Zane Grey reading public had been found," says Frank Luther Mott in his history of bestsellers, "one of his books could be expected to sell around a half million copies over a series of years." Some titles, such as *Riders of the Purple Sage*, sold several times that figure. One of the chief activities of the country from World War I on was consuming Zane Grey material in one shape or other. A goodly number of people were kept occupied in converting Grey novels into new and even more palatable forms. The silent-movie folks loved Zane Grey. Tom Mix starred in adaptations of the novels; so did Richard Dix and Jack Holt. When the talkies came, almost everything Zane Grey had written was turned into a movie, many A-productions and scores of Bs. Newspaper syndicates had discovered Zane Grey fairly early. His novels were frequently serialized in the 1920s. In the 1930s several of the books—*Nevada* was one such—were turned into short-run comic strips. It took Stephen Slesinger to come up with a longer-lasting Zane Grey strip. He sold *King of the Royal Mounted* by Zane Grey to King Features in 1935. I suppose this is technically a Northern not a Western, but we'll stick it here anyway. The middle thirties was the period when Edgar Wallace, Frank Buck, and Eddie Rickenbacker were also supposedly writing adventure strips. Grey, like Edgar Wallace on *Inspector Wade*, was able to keep writing the strip for several years after his death. Canadian Mountie King, like Talbot Mundy's earlier King of the Khyber Rifles, was really

named King. It was not an honorary title like, say, Benny Good-
man's appellation the King of Swing.

The first artist on the strip was Allen Dean, who drew in a stocky,
drybrush pulp style. The Lone Ranger's mask was the test of a man's
mettle in that strip; with King the big challenge was his wide,
flat-brimmed Mountie hat. Basically what you had to do was draw
a plate with an inverted bowl sitting on it, and show it from every
possible angle. Dean never could get it right. Since none of the sur-
vivors of the 1930s King Features bullpen whom I've talked to can
remember anything about Allen Dean, it's probable he worked
directly for Slesinger. For a brief spell he also drew *Tex Thorne,* a
Sunday page credited to Zane Grey. In the spring of 1938 Dean left
the RCMP strip (He'd dropped the Sunday in 1936), and dependable
Charles Flanders drew it until he changed horsemen and assumed
the *Lone Ranger.* Jim Gary then became the *King of the Royal
Mounted* artist.

Thirty-four when he became responsible for Sergeant King, Jim
Gary had led the sort of life all rugged novelists used to claim in
their dust-jacket autobiographies. He'd been a merchant seaman,
worked as a dishwasher, herded cattle in Arizona, taken flying lessons in Australia, and ridden across America on a motorcycle. In the
late 1930s Gary settled down some and began to draw for the Whitman line of comic books. Working in a style that was an inade-
quately blended hash of Raymond and Caniff, Gary turned out pages
about G-men, cowboys, and detectives for *Crackajack Funnies* and
Popular Comics. He'd improved considerably by the time Slesinger
gave him his turn with the Mountie. Eventually the burden of doing
his own strip and ghosting *Red Ryder* now and then apparently
became too much for Gary, so he got other artists to ghost *King* for
him. Among them was Rodlow Willard, onetime gag cartoonist,
who later served eight years on *Scorchy Smith.*

Although Sergeant King was as dedicated as any Royal Canadian
Mounted Policeman when it came to getting his man, some of the
men he got during the Jim Gary years were a cut above the villainous trapper and crazed Indian most fictional Mounties went
after. King chased deranged doctors who dressed up in winged suits
and called themselves the Black Bat, tonsured inventors who
prowled the coastal waters of British Columbia in mysterious subma-
rines, homicidal acrobats, hooded terrors, and lady Robin Hoods. In
the majority of his cases he was accompanied by a boy called Kid.

A handsome example of Garrett Price's White Boy. © *1933 New York News Syndicate Co., Inc. Reprinted by permission.*

The best drawn, and least seen, Western strip of the thirties was Garrett Price's *White Boy*. This Sunday page began in the early 1930s, distributed by the Chicago Tribune-New York News Syndicate. Price, once employed in the *Tribune* art department, thinks it was the syndicate which came to him with the idea of doing a strip. "I was hampered by authentic knowledge of the West," Price told me. "My folks (Papa was a doctor) left Kansas when I was a year old. Until I was nineteen we lived in Wyoming, Oklahoma and South Dakota—mostly in Wyoming." Originally set in the past, the page dealt with an adolescent boy who is captured by the Sioux and then rescued by a rival tribe. White Boy is befriended by an Indian girl named Starlight, and by two young braves, Chickadee and Woodchuck. The pages were drawn in a gentle style, quite different in appearance from what Price was doing for the *New Yorker*. "A style at once decorative, tender, and with a true feeling for the

191

open air," is how Coulton Waugh described it. "The stories had an imaginative, dreamy character." Price was continually experimenting, breaking up the page into all sorts of patterns. Sometimes he used the conventional twelve-panel layout, but more often tried things like using one huge panel bordered by two or three long thin ones. His rendering got bolder, poster-like. His color, alternating harsh basic reds with subdued autumnal pastels, was unlike anything being done on the comic pages. The feature did not collect a sizable audience. By 1934 *White Boy* had moved to the present, to a place called Skull Valley. The title was changed shortly thereafter to *Skull Valley;* the dreamy stories and Indian folktales gave way to galloping outlaws and masked heroes. In spite of the new story material, Price was incapable of doing a conventional job. His melodramatic pages, rich with thick black and villainous greens and yellows, still stood out from *The Gumps* and *Winnie Winkle.* In 1936 the page was dropped. "Captain Joe Patterson thought the story was not carrying over from week to week," recalls Price. "It was suggested that I make it a daily, too. As it was, even once a week was getting to be a grind, the episodes harder and harder to think up. Things at the *New Yorker* were picking up, the depression was easing. Still I made one last try. For new material I looked for a new field, went to Mexico." When he returned, rather than go on with *Skull Valley* at all, Price quit and concentrated on magazine cartooning and illustrating, something much closer to his heart. Price, a small, modest man, would just as well let his Sunday page remain unsung and unremembered. "If there is anything I wish to be remembered for, it is not for being an unsuccessful comic-strip artist."

Funny-paper cowboys had become movie and serial heroes, but the process could be worked the other way as well. This resulted in comic strips about such screen cowboys as Tom Mix and Gene Autry. In the middle 1930s Tom Mix, who had been playing cowboys in the movies since 1911, was a declining screen hero. He still had his Rolls Royce, he even had a cowboy-style tuxedo, but things were not as good as they had been. Then the Ralston Company of Checkerboard Square, St. Louis, Missouri, bought Tom Mix. They created a club, named it the Tom Mix Ralston Straight Shooters. They put on a *Tom Mix* radio show, with an actor doing Tom, and got a cartoonist to do a comic strip. Tom Mix was popular again. The Sunday page, with *advertisement* printed above it, ran once a month or so—one of the few Western strips which gave you both

Even under a more melodramatic title, Price's page looked like nobody else's. © 1935 Chicago Tribune–New York News Syndicate, Inc. Reprinted by permission.

Wild West adventure and nutritional advice. And the Sunday page was where you really got to know Tom. The most intimate glimpse came in a strip offering an exact wooden replica of a six-shooter just like Tom's for 10 cents and one Ralston box top. Along with the picture of the gun and a photo of Tom was a diagram of Tom Mix's injuries. "Tom Mix has been blown up once, shot twelve times and injured forty-seven times in movie stunting. This chart shows the location of some of Tom's injuries (X marks fractures; circles bullet wounds)." My favorite wound was L: "Shot through elbow in real stage coach hold-up (1902)."

Gene Autry, a Texas boy, had been singing cowboy songs over the radio when he was given the lead in a serial entitled *Phantom Empire*. The serial, one of the few cowboy science fiction stories ever filmed, brought Autry to the attention of Republic studios. They cast him in *Tumbling Tumbleweeds*. Besides shooting his gun and riding his horse, the double-chinned cowpoke also sang. The box-office reaction to this led to the quick emergence of a new type of hero, the singing cowboy. A fairly shrewd businessman, Autry soon went into the business of merchandising himself. One of the by-products was *Gene Autry Rides!* A Sunday page, it was written by Gerald Geraghty and drawn by Till Goodan. Goodan, another cowboy turned cartoonist, was better at horses and saddles than he was at people. Gene Autry never sang in the strip.

Chapter 11
The Boys in Uniform

IN THIS COUNTRY we've had military heroes as presidents, as university officials, and even as movie actors, but there's never been a really successful comic strip featuring a hero in uniform. Which may indicate that people are more demanding and discriminating about entertainment than they are about real life. It is true that during the Second World War Terry, Smilin' Jack, Joe Palooka, and sundry other strip leads were in the service, but they were all characters who had already gained popularity as civilians. The heroes who began their careers in full uniform in the thirties and forties, men like Don Winslow, Stony Craig, and Navy Bob Steele, never made it to the top of any of the popularity lists. Starting off as a military-adventure-strip star in the 1930s was especially difficult, since a good many of the paying customers didn't want to be reminded about anything pertaining to war and battle—certainly not battles that were going to involve our own soldiers, sailors, and marines. Watching a grinning Errol Flynn riding bravely off to the Little Big Horn or charging with the Light Brigade was about as close as most people then wanted to get to a shooting war.

The most successful character in the uncrowded field of serviceman strips was Don Winslow. The *Don Winslow of the Navy* feature, initially as a daily strip only, appeared in the spring of 1934. From the start it was mixed entertainment with propaganda, one of its principal purposes being to encourage enlistments in the Navy. Winslow's creator was Frank V. Martinek. A former Navy Intelligence officer and newspaper reporter, Martinek was at that time a personnel executive with Standard Oil of Indiana. Since he still held a commission in the Naval Reserve, he was able to sign himself Lt. Commander F. V. Martinek on the strip. According to accounts Martinek later gave out, he decided to invent Don Winslow when he heard the Navy was having a difficult time recruiting sailors in the Midwest. Martinek figured an adventure strip about a Navy man would give landlocked youths a taste of the sea and, hopefully, push some of them toward signing up. He was a friend of Col. Frank Knox, the publisher of the *Chicago Daily News,* and Knox in turn was a friend and hunting crony of Jack Wheeler of Bell Syndicate. Bell contracted to handle *Don Winslow of the Navy.*

Knox, who was Alf Landon's running mate in the presidential race of 1936, was appointed Secretary of the Navy by FDR in 1940. I haven't been able to determine whether he had any other qualifications for the job beyond his early involvement with *Don Winslow.*

Martinek served as the mastermind, for want of a better word, behind the new strip. Most of the actual work was done by others. "One day two artists came into my office," he later told an interviewer. "Leon A. Beroth and Carl E. Hammond. Why they came I cannot explain, but it seemed Providence was getting us together." As Martinek explained the working setup, he was the producer, Beroth the art director, and Hammond the layout and research man. For some reason Hammond never got a credit on the strip during all the years he worked on it, although by the middle thirties he was writing as well as laying out the thing.

The initial episodes of the *Winslow* saga brought not only salt water but insidious villainy to its readers. Right off the bat Don tangled with the Scorpion, "leader of an international gang of plotters." Martinek was preoccupied with preparedness and with the infiltration of America by foreign agents. Almost all his villains, from the thirties on into the first months of the Second World War, were spies and saboteurs of one sort or other. The Scorpion was the most recurrent of the batch. A sinister, baldheaded fellow, looking somewhat like a hairless Lionel Atwill, it was "his mad dream to one day rule the world." Winslow was also pitted against such scoundrels as the Crocodile, who flew through the air in an immense

An early warning to would-be invaders, almost a year before Pearl Harbor. This page is one Ken Ernst worked on. Released 1941 Bell Syndicate. Reprinted by permission.

contraption called Sky-City and was killing U. S. sailors in the South Seas by dropping hollow ice cubes full of poison gas on them; Dr. Q, one of the many thirties villains bent on destroying the Panama Canal; Dr. Centaur, who'd invented "the weirdest weapon in the world." There were also the Duchess, Owl-eyes, Dr. Thor, and the Dwarf. When captured the Dwarf warns Don what the international spies have in mind. America is, he explains, "the most fertile of all fields for spies. . . . I tell you they'll flood your land with secret agents—spying out your military secrets, undermining your people's faith in their leaders." This surprises Don, who asks, "But why?" "Among all the world powers is there none who would pay them well for crippling America's strength? Think it over, Winslow!"

Lt. Commander Winslow, as Martinek had been during World War I, was with Naval Intelligence. This gave him considerable mobility, and if a continuity sagged an order from Washington could rush him into an entirely new adventure. Don was accompanied, almost always, by an assistant named Lt. Red Pennington. Apparently the Navy had no weight limits for its men in those days, since Red was a huge, pudgy fellow almost twice as wide as his superior. Something of a throwback to the fat sidekick of boys' adventure books, Red was much given to such expressions as "Horsefeathers!" and "Holy smoke!" It wasn't all falling out of dirigibles and saving the Panama Canal; there was also romance in Don Winslow's life. While he dallied now and then with the various lovely lady spies who frequented the strip, his real love was Mercedes Colby. Mercedes, who grew continually better looking as the artwork improved, was the daughter of an admiral and the niece of another one, Admiral Warburton, who was Don's boss. She first showed up in the *Winslow* panels in 1935 and by 1941 was in the Navy herself, as a nurse. Don finally reached the point, in December of 1941, where he proposed to the girl. But another assignment interfered, and then the war caught up with the continuity. By February of 1942 Don and Red were on their way to fight the Japanese in the Pacific.

In 1935 a Sunday *Don Winslow* page was added, as well as a companion half-page given over to the adventures of *Bos'n Hal, Sea Scout.* Hal, an extremely clean-cut lad, spent much less time with spies and infiltrators than Don. His specialty was going on treasure hunts to remote spots. Toward the end of the decade Bell considered introducing a daily *Bos'n Hal* strip. Several sample weeks were produced, but nothing came of the project. Hal sank from sight altogether before the war.

As a newspaper feature *Don Winslow of the Navy* never earned enough to pay a decent salary to the staff of men producing it. As a merchandising property, however, it was a palpable hit. In addition to the usual comic-book reprints and Big Little Books, there was also a series of hardcover juvenile novels based on Don Winslow's far-flung intrigues. More lucrative was the network radio serial (with "Columbia, the Gem of the Ocean" as its theme song), which took to the air in the late thirties, sponsored by Kellogg. The first Don was an actor named Bob Guilbert, followed by Raymond Edward Johnson (Raymond of "Inner Sanctum"). John Gibson, who made a career of playing sidekicks on radio, was the most frequent Red. Universal turned out two thirteen-chapter *Winslow* serials, in 1941 and 1943, both of which pitted Don against the Scorpion. Don Terry, a clunky middle-aged-banker type, portrayed Commander Winslow. The Scorpion was assayed first by Kurt Katch and then by that brilliant second-rate character actor Nestor Paiva. There was also, fleetingly, a *Don Winslow* pulp magazine, but this apparently was unauthorized.

As the affluence produced by merchandising continued, the *Don Winslow* strip itself got better looking. Hammond and Beroth were able to hire more people to lend a hand. Among them was Ed Moore, whom we met last as a *Dan Dunn* assistant. Moore joined them in their small office, which he remembers as being "about twenty feet deep and a couple windows wide." He did backgrounds and lettering on the *Winslow* strip, penciled the entire *Bos'n Hal* page. It was also Moore who did the sample strips for the projected *Bos'n Hal* daily. Moore was concurrently doing comic-book work. His spare Chicago-style pages, very effectively designed, stand out among those of many of his more clumsy funny-book contemporaries. Since he never drew a superhero, the wave of enthusiasm which has swept much of the so-called Golden Age material back into prominence hasn't touched Ed Moore's work. But his *Manhunter, Spy, Jack Wander,* and others are very good, very individual. Shortly before the commencement of World War II Moore achieved a Sunday page of his own. Most of the work on the *Winslow* strip fell, thereafter, to Ken Ernst.

Like Moore, Ernst had studied at the Chicago Academy of Fine Arts and drawn for comic books. But he had different idols. Kenneth Frederic Ernst was born in 1918. "This singular event took place in the little coal-mining town of Stanton, Illinois, at the height of the worst snow storm in the history of the state," he has said. "By the time I was six my folks had settled on Chicago's West Side." His father ran a delicatessen, which was just around the corner from the garage where, in 1929, the St. Valentine's Day Massacre took place. As Ernst recalls, several of the Bugs Moran mobsters killed that day were good customers of his father's. It was his father who financed a mail-order cartoon course for him. "Then I was on my way." By the time he was twelve, however, he had also become fascinated with magic. "I actually performed for pay in my teens," he says. "Some cartoons I did for the local magic club magazine caught the eye of a fellow magician who was a commercial artist by profession, and he persuaded me to take up the study of art and cartooning seriously." Ernst started attending the Chicago Art Institute days and the Academy of Fine Art, by night. He then got his first professional cartooning job, working as assistant to an artist named Nick Nichols on a less than good fantasy strip titled *Peter Pen.*

Nichols's minimal abilities didn't stop him from running a cartoon school; for a time Ernst taught there.

In the mid-1930s Ernst discovered the work of Milton Caniff and Noel Sickles. His sister, working as an artist's model in New York, was occasionally hired by Caniff and Sickles. And Ernst visited their Tudor City studio a few times. Ernst is the one who brought the Caniff-Sickles views back to Chicago, where their style eventually infected a good many others, including almost everyone who was to work for the Publishers Syndicate. It's also evident from looking at Ken Ernst's drawing from the late thirties that he picked up a good deal from studying Mel Graff's stuff. Ernst's approach to layout and the basic heroic male head he favored owe considerable to Graff. Out of all the borrowings and imitations, though, Ernst developed a loose, splashy style of his own. He sold his first comic-book pages in 1936. By 1939 he was working for several of the major outfits. For the *Superman* people's *Detective Comics* he did private eye *Larry Steele*. For Vincent Sullivan's splendidly named *Big Shot Comics* he did *Tom Kerry*, a D.A. with private eye tendencies. These were for New York City companies. Ernst journeyed as well up to Racine to sell Whitman several features, the most notable being a combination jungle man-magician name of *Magic Morro*. Ernst even illustrated Big Little Books, specializing in cowboy heroes Tom Mix and Buck Jones.

Ernst got married about this time. Deciding he needed an extra and, hopefully, more steady job, he joined Beroth and Hammond in 1940. This position still wasn't paying much, so he kept all his other freelance jobs going. "At one time I spent mornings penciling all the *Winslow* and *Bos'n Hal* art, afternoons at a Chicago art-agency doing advertising strips, and topped off the day by working all evening on my own comic-book creations."

The whole appearance of *Winslow* changed. Ernst brought to *Don Winslow* not only techniques assimilated from Graff and Caniff, but also the more extravagant layouts he's developed in the comic books. By the end of 1940 the strip had lost its cartoony appearance. Long shots, close-ups, and other movie-type setups became frequent. Ernst was especially fond of shooting up from floor level and, as Orson Welles was about to do in the movies, showing the ceiling. He staged action much better than most of his predecessors. The strip, during Ernst's nearly two years with it, was attractive, but the fact that it was done in a hurry often showed—there was a sloppy, batted-out quality to much of the work. After Ernst left, Leon

200

Beroth struggled, with assorted help and varied results, to keep *Winslow* looking the way he had when Ernst drew him. Don Winslow served in a variety of war zones, once even working in drag to serve his country. After World War II his adventures and his circulation grew more modest. Most of the merchandising money stopped, though the movie serials did run as a show in the watch-anything-that-moves days of television. Bell dropped the strip in 1952, and the less prestigious General Features Syndicate took over distribution. When the strip ceased in 1955, neither Beroth or Hammond was associated with it, the drawing being by comic-book graduate John Jordan.

In the thirties, Jack Wheeler's Bell Syndicate seemingly wouldn't rest until a hero from every branch of the service had been tried. They got around to the Marine Corps in the fall of 1937, when they introduced *Sergeant Stony Craig.* "Stony Craig is the typical Marine Sergeant . . . hard-boiled, tough, a disciplinarian, but underneath, a great fellow and soldier," said the promotion copy by way of introduction. "With his group of Marines, he hits some strange adventure and exciting action . . . on land, at sea, in the air, the Marines keep the situation well in hand." The new daily was the work of two career Marines, Sgt. Frank H. Rentfrow and Lt. Don L. Dickson. Rentfrow, a pulp writer and former editor of *Leatherneck,* provided the continuity. Dickson, a reserve officer and commercial artist, did the drawing. The drawing lieutenant, one of whose "proudest boasts is that he is an expert rifle shot," worked in a simple-minded outline style, and his Stony Craig looked like a schoolboy's copy of Captain Easy. Since this was still peacetime, Stony and his Marines limited their combat to situations other than battle. They might, for example, be ordered to Alaska on "a secret and dangerous mission," or become embroiled in the political problems of the tiny European country of Littenburg.

After nearly three years the strip still had less than fifty client papers. Nevertheless, a Sunday page was added in June of 1940. The topper was called *Daredevils of Destiny.* Subtitled "True Stories of Gallant Men," it was much more openly gung ho about the Marines than the *Stony Craig* strip. To avoid charges that they had any other motive than providing entertainment, Rentfrow and Dickson always made it perfectly clear, in syndicate press releases and interviews, "that the strip contains no propaganda for the Marine Corps." At the close of 1940 Dickson was recalled to active duty. Rentfrow continued to write the feature, using an assortment of artists. Bill

SERGEANT STONY CRAIG—Blade Goes Peaceably
By Frank H. Rentfrow and Don L. Dickson

Sergeant Stony Craig *had clunky art, but lots of action.* © 1938 Bell Syndicate, Inc. Reprinted by permission.

Draut was one of them. Draut picked up the strip as the war was ending, doing it in an extremely simplified version of the Caniff style. Characteristically, Sergeant Stony went on fighting the Japanese for several months after the offical shutoff of the Second World War.

A couple of years before the Marines landed on the comic page, Bell Syndicate had offered an Army strip of sorts. *Wiley of West*

Point by Lt. Richard Rick would surely win a place near the top of any list of the ten most dreadful adventure strips of all time. The drawing and writing, both seemingly the work of Lt. Rick himself, were godawful. It's difficult not to suspect that Wheeler was pressured or threatened into taking on such a strip at all. The first day began with an invocation, "A story dedicated to those who have by service to the nation inspired all Americans with the highest sense of duty," and then got down to the business of following young Bob Wiley as he leaves his small-town home to enter West Point. Such is young Bob's anxiety to get into uniform that when the bus he's riding breaks down, he hires a plane and parachutes out over the parade ground. His enthusiasm was not catching. The strip soon expired.

Just about every kind of uniform was tried on in the thirties, including the Boy Scout uniform. *Roy Powers, Eagle Scout* was a product of the Ledger Syndicate. Labeled the "Official story of the Boy Scouts of America," this daily was credited to Paul Powell. Paul Powell was actually a group of people, comprising writer Paul Roberts and whatever Ledger artist happened to be handy. During his several years as an Eagle Scout, Roy's adventures were illuminated by Kemp Starrett, Jimmy Thompson, and Frank Godwin. The longest term of service was put in by Godwin, and since he was doing *Connie* at the same time, he never put his name to the Scout strip. Roy was a tall handsome lad, in the Charles Dana Gibson tradition. He had the requisite fat friend—Chunky, this one's name was. Never hindered by obligations to school or family, Roy Powers wandered the world year-round. He hunted lions in Africa, tackled crazed inventors and airline hijackers closer to home. This was very much a boy's strip, probably intended for kids a few years younger than Roy and Chunky. While there was a good deal of action and comradery, there were practically no girls. This must have been disappointing to Frank Godwin. His specialty, after horses, was certainly pretty girls.

The McClure Syndicate launched a Navy feature late in 1939, with a real Navy man providing the script. The new Sunday page, *Navy Bob Steele*, was written by Lt. Wilson Starbuck, U.S.N.R., and drawn by Erwin Greenwood. The initial half-page appeared on November 5, the same day as the first *Superman* half-page, with the syndicate hoping newspapers would buy them both as a package deal. According to McClure publicity, "many of the incidents were inspired by active service experiences of Lt. Starbuck, who at the age of 19 won a commission and was placed in command of US Submarine Chaser No. 20 at New York in 1917. During the war he also

ROY POWERS, EAGLE SCOUT— The Cobra Strikes

ROY POWERS, EAGLE SCOUT— Danger in Wait!

Four Roy Powers dailies, demonstrating that Boy Scout life was not all knot-tying and helping little old ladies across streets. All drawn by Frank Godwin. © Ledger Syndicate.

ROY POWERS, EAGLE SCOUT— Quick Change for Cairo

THEIR PLANE'S FUEL EXHAUSTED AND THE FIELD FLOODLIGHTS OUT OF ORDER, AN ALMOST CERTAIN CRASH WAS AVERTED WHEN ROY MADE PARACHUTE LIGHTS FROM THE MAGNESIUM FLARES IN THEIR CAMERA EQUIPMENT —

L-25

WELL, WE'RE DOWN - AND ALL IN ONE PIECE

THAT WAS A GRAND BIT OF QUICK THINKING, ROY, MAKING THOSE FLARES

YOU SAY IT'S WAITING AT THE AIRWAYS DOCK? - RIGHT - WE'LL BE THERE IN 10 MINUTES -

COME ON, BOYS - WE CAN GET A TAXI AT THE GATE - THE SEA PLANE IS WAITING TO FLY US TO CAIRO

ROY POWERS, EAGLE SCOUT— Air-Liner Robbery

LOOK, PHIL! DO YOU SEE THOSE LIGHTS ON THE GROUND?

I'LL SAY I DO! THIS THING GETS CRAZIER BY THE MINUTE!

N-13

THOSE ARE PORTABLE LANDING FLOODLIGHTS IF I EVER SAW 'EM! THIS BUSINESS IS ORGANIZED!

WE BETTER NOTIFY THE AIR LINE, DON'T YOU THINK?

ALL RIGHT - CLIMB OUT, EVERYBODY, WITH YOUR HANDS UP - AND DON'T TRY NO TRICKS!

WHILE ON THE GROUND, IN THE GLARE OF THE FLOODLIGHTS, A STRANGE SCENE TAKES PLACE

served on the USS Shawmut and engaged in mine laying in the North Sea. After the Armistice he was transferred to the air detachment of the Atlantic Fleet." Probably more significant, as far as the strip was concerned, was the dashingly named Lt. Starbuck's job during the Second World War. He was a public relations officer.

The *Navy Bob* page in the years immediately before Pearl Harbor featured "Lt. Robert Steele, USN, known since his football days as 'Navy Bob Steele.'" Plus Bob's "classmate, team-mate and brother officer Lt. 'Bill' Sheridan"; Tommy Andrews, gunner's mate 1st class and "a boy from the same town and a graduate of the same high school as Lt. Steele"; and "Red" Malone, seaman 1st class and "pal of Tommy's." The physical format of the Sunday page was close to that of *Don Winslow*, down to the final panel devoted to Navy lore. Readers were invited to "clip and save for your Navy scrapbook," such items as "Sometimes dirigibles anchor at sea. Here is a man who has just finished inspecting the anchor of one far above him," and "The Navy makes sure its parachutes are in good shape. Here they are being aired and inspected." The adventures of Navy Bob were somewhat more exciting than that. When the war broke out he went to the Pacific, where he spent his time slaughtering Japanese. The war lasted longer than he did.

On Sunday, September 7, 1941, a new Sunday page made its appearance. *Biff Baker* by Henry Lee had for its hero a young man who was a "college senior, football star and amateur aviator." Lee had a four-square illustrator's style, giving the impression he'd moved into comics from advertising. Two months before the bombing of Pearl Harbor was not the best time to introduce a college football star who dabbled in flying. Some changes were made, and by early 1942 Lee had Biff capturing a Nazi spy ring (led by a chap with a Von Stroheim shaved head and monocle) which was attempting to flourish on campus. In June Biff graduated from Midwestern University and, through the intercession of an influential uncle, went into the Air Corps. When Biff hears this news he exclaims, "Oh, boy, that's great! Uncle Jim, you're a wonder!" By shifting focus between Biff and some of his chums, Lee managed to cover the war in both the Pacific and Europe. His Japanese were, to a man, cunning and fiendish devils who delighted in delivering the kind of tooth-sucking lines Richard Loo was getting off in the movies: "I will take gun! I insist on pleasure of shooting American and hearing him beg for mercy!" As the forties progressed, Henry Lee left the page, possibly to go into the service himself. NEA kept his name on it, which couldn't have done his reputation any good since the ghost artist was pixie-loving Walt Scott. Scott, as you may recall, was also botching the *Captain Easy* Sunday page during this period.

Even before the U.S. entry into World War II the draft had started, building up something known as the peacetime Army. Some of the minor cultural side-effects were comedy films like Bob Hope's *Caught in the Draft* and Abbott and Costello's *Buck Privates*, and a new comic strip called *Draftie*. Credited to Paul Fogarty, the strip was drawn by several different artists. Longest on the job was William Juhré, last seen drawing *Tarzan*. Draftie, that was his only name, was a small-town rube from Cider City. His Army career was another enactment of the country boy amid the slickers. Soon teamed up with a little Brooklyn hotshot named Oinie, Draftie's maiden adventures took him through the then unfamiliar routines of induction and basic training. For a while Fogarty and Juhré aimed for a joke, or reasonable facsimile, every day. When the real war began there was a swing toward straighter continuities. Never a subtle piece of work, *Draftie* was another war strip which destroyed enemy soldiers, both Germans and Japanese, with chuckling exuberance. Although the copy was never much, Juhré did some interesting drawing. He modified his illustrational style considerably as the forties unrolled, apparently the only comic-strip artist influenced by Britain's David Low.

United Feature's entry into the uniformed ranks came as the war was starting. The strip was *Race Riley of the Commandos*, drawn by Milburn Rosser. It concerned itself with American Riley's service in a British raiding unit, a Yank-in-the-commandos sort of thing. Race Riley's military career was unconventional even for a commando. After a raid or two, he undertook to work with the underground in occupied France. The fact that he was an American through and through, no matter what sort of uniform or disguise he put on, was emphasized by his speech patterns. "Sizzlin' sassafras!" Race would cry out in moments of stress. He was also fond of "What's cookin'?" and he never said "you" when he could substitute "ya." While the Gestapo is closing in on him, Race radios England to report, "I'm hotter'n a firecracker in this burg!" A former pulp illustrator and concocter of Sunday ad strips for such products as Camel Cigarettes, Rosser was a journeyman artist, competent but dull.

His Race Riley, despite his slangy talk, was a blond, clean-cut young man of the sort who always leaned over to light the girl's cigarette in the Camel ads.

The next hero had a uniform, but a uniform like nobody else. A black airplane helmet with scarlet goggle straps he wore, a midnight-blue flying suit trimmed in gold with a winged clock on the breast of the tunic. Cap . . . tain. . . . Midnight! First a Chicago-born radio-serial hero, Captain Midnight rapidly branched out into graphics. As with other mythical and mysterious characters, there was some disagreement as to what the captain looked like. In his first comic-book incarnation, in *The Funnies* in 1941, he was decked out in a brown leather flying jacket and crimson scarf. In his second comic-book go-round, in the Fawcett magazine bearing his name, he inclined more toward the superhero in dress. The reason the Midnight character showed up in so many different places is that he was a property—a property of the Wander Company, makers of Ovaltine, who were intent on merchandising him and his Secret Squadron as much as possible. The rights to turn Captain Midnight into a newspaper strip were peddled around by the Ovaltine folks. At one time the Chicago Tribune-New York News Syndicate was interested and approached several artists about drawing a proposed strip. Among them was young John Dirks, already assisting his father with his version of the *Katzenjammer* saga. Eventually the Chicago Sun Syndicate bought the rights to use the captain in the funny papers. The name Jonwan was the only credit ever given on the strip, but it's obvious that the production of the newspaper *Captain Midnight* was done by people associated with Whitman's Big Little Book division. The artist who did the greater portion of the drawing was Erwin L. Hess, with Henry Vallely and a couple of others backing him up. Hess, more recently involved with a nostalgia panel done in a deliberately antiquated style, was working in the Caniff vein in the early forties. People were not his strong suit, a fact he compensated for by filling his pages with effectively done landscapes and imposing scenes of ships, planes, trains, castles, European cities. For some reason *Captain Midnight* was available as a full page, and many of these giant-size drawings of Hess' are quite impressive. He was able to get coloring equal to that on *Terry*, utilizing, for instance, what looks to be a dozen or more shades of red and yellow for a sequence showing the captain and his sidekick Ikky flying over an autumn forest. The scripts were nowhere near as colorful, although an illusive and recurrent villainess known as the Moon Woman was ambiguous enough to be interesting. The Secret Squadron, turning its back on radio villains like Ivan Shark, gave over the war years to combat with the Nazis.

While none of the military strips we've examined was appreciably successful, the object they'd been created for was reached anyway. The advent of the war took care of that. There was no more problem about filling the ranks of the Army, Navy, and Marines. This was to be the last war where a majority of the people believed in the necessity of fighting. Even the comic-strip heroes were joining up. Terry Lee, Pat Ryan, Joe Palooka, Sparky Watts, Smilin' Jack, Harold Teen, and Skeezix volunteered. Even Clark Kent tried to enlist. Combat, bombing, and killing became a familiar part of the comic-page content—combat, bombing, killing, and propaganda. The end of the war didn't mean the end of any of that.

And we might as well finish with a Minute Movies *clinch.*

Suggestions For Further Reading (& Looking):
A Subjectively Annotated Source List

Those of you who've read along with me from start to finish probably realize that I don't think very highly of most of the general histories of the comic-strip field (with the exception of Waugh's *The Comics*). But if you want a sparse sampling of some of the adventure strips we've talked about, don't let me keep you away from the various catchall chronicles. What I've put together below is a list of sources for more extended samplings of adventure strips. Obviously the better-known strips are the ones which have been most frequently reprinted and enshrined.

Chap. 1: WHAT THE . . . ?

Little Nemo

For those who want to go back this far in time, Woody Gelman has put together a large-size and handsome collection of the earliest Winsor McCay Sunday pages (many in color). Available from his Nostalgia Press. (This and other pertinent addresses will be found in a lump at the end of this section.)

An exceptional bargain is Dover's recent paperback reprint of McCay's *Dreams of the Rarebit Fiend.* Not an adventure strip, but quite impressive and entertaining.

Hairbreadth Harry

Kahles's version has never been reprinted in any quantity. F. O. Alexander's Sunday pages from the 1930s can be found in the first few years of *Famous Funnies.* (Bob Overstreet's *Comic Book Price Guide* will give you information on this title and the sundry other comic books which reprinted newspaper strips.)

Minute Movies

As yet there is no book reprinting Wheelan's work. Gelman ran a sequence in issues 2 and 3 of his *Nostalgia Comics,* but these were 1930s strips ghosted by Afonsky. Wheelan, as mentioned, revived his feature for *Flash Comics* in the early 1940s. However, this is also a superhero title, with some of the *Minute Movies* issues selling for as much as $40 at the moment.

The Gumps

This strip is most readily available in two slipshod books thrown together by Herb Galewitz. *The Gumps* (Scribner's, 1974) is made up entirely of the talky dailies. *Great Comics* (Crown, 1972) offers a short run of badly reproduced daily strips. It was in the Sunday page, starring Chester Gump, that the real adventuring went on. These were reprinted in *Popular* and *Super Comics* (check Overstreet).

Chap. 2: LICKETY WHOP!

Wash Tubbs/Captain Easy

Gordon Campbell and Jim Ivey have compiled a book of the most interesting 1920s Tubbs adventures (Luna Press, 1974). Alan Light's weekly reprint tabloid, *Vintage Funnies,* is currently reprinting *Easy* Sundays from the late thirties.

Chap. 3: TARZAN EVERY SUNDAY

Tarzan

The most economical source of *Tarzan,* daily and Sunday, is the series of softcover reprints being issued by the House of Greystoke. Both early dailies and Maxon, Foster, and Hogarth Sunday pages have been reprinted (all Sundays in black-and-white, however). Various European publishers have reprinted the pages in full color, but translated into their respective languages. *Tarzan* appeared in *Tip Top Comics, Sparkler* and *Comics On Parade* in the thirties and forties. The *Menomonee Falls Gazette* is running the current Russ Manning *Tarzan* and the resurrected dailies (by Dan Barry, Nick Cardy, etc.).

Prince Valiant

Nostalgia Press has brought forth color reprints of the early pages. Foreign-edition plates from recolored and diddled-with Sundays were used, though, making for a blurry overall look.

The Phantom

Nostalgia Press has one book of Ray Moore's ungainly dailies available. The present day *Ghost Who Walks* strip (as well as Falk's *Mandrake*) can be found in the weekly *Menomonee Falls Gazette*.

Chap. 4: THAT BUCK ROGERS STUFF

Buck Rogers

The biggest and cheapest source is that prince of remainders, *The Collected Works of Buck Rogers* (Chelsea House, 1969).

Brick Bradford

The old redhead's early adventures are on view in *Nostalgia Comics*. Today's strip, by Paul Norris, can be followed in the *Menomonee Falls Gazette*.

Jack Swift

If you must look at this thing, there is a Big Little Book entitled *Jack Swift and His Rocket Ship* (Whitman, 1934).

Flash Gordon

The first two Nostalgia Press collections, which used black-and-white proofs to work from, are by far the best looking.

Don Dixon

The pages are being reprinted in *Vintage Funnies*.

Chap. 5: GANGBUSTERS

Dick Tracy

Another perennial remainder is *The Celebrated Cases of Dick Tracy* (Bonanza, 1970). For more of Dick's 1930s cases, see *Vintage Funnies*.

Secret Agent X-9

The earliest Austin Briggs dailies can be found in *Nostalgia*

Comics 4 and 5. Captain George's Vast Whizzbang Organization reprinted the first Raymond sequences, but that particular publication is no longer in print. The new improved *X-9* is in the pages of the *Menomonee Falls Gazette*.

Charlie Chan

In the late thirties and early forties the Andriola strip was reprinted in *Feature Comics* and *Big Shot Comics*. It's rumored a collection is in the works in Europe.

Jim Hardy

About the only source of reprints is the old *Tip Top Comics* and the half-dozen or so one-shot *Jim Hardy* magazines (again see Overstreet). At least one semi-pro publisher wants to do a book of Moores's strip, but has been unable to locate a run to reprint from (the syndicate does not have proofs of the early years of the feature).

Chap. 6: "BEEN AROUND THE WORLD IN A PLANE, SETTLED REVOLUTIONS IN SPAIN"

Tailspin Tommy

Looking at too much of Hal Forrest's dreadful artwork may be hazardous to your health. The old Sunday pages are being rerun in *Vintage Funnies*.

Skyroads

The late Ed Aprill published a book of the very early dailies a few years back. Copies still seem to be available from some of the specialty dealers. Keaton's version ran in *Famous Funnies*.

Smilin' Jack

There were various comic-book reprints of Jack's airplane adventures. A smattering of 1930s dailies and Sundays appear in the above-mentioned *Great Comics*. Be warned, however, that these were printed up from out-of-focus microfilm and they'll make you airsick if you look at them for very long.

Barney Baxter

Comic-book reprints are the only place to find Barney and Gopher Gus.

Scorchy Smith

Sickles's dailies, badly reproduced, ran in *Famous Funnies*. Christman's stuff fared a bit better, although it was relettered. The issue of *Action Comics* which introduced Christman's *3 Aces* is selling for between $60 and $120, so you'd better skip that unless you're extremely curious.

Chap. 7: TERRY AND THE PIRATES

Nostalgia Press has a fine volume of the first year of Caniff dailies. *Vintage Funnies* has been reprinting the strip, daily and Sunday, from mid-1938 onward.

Chap. 8: GLORYOSKY!

Little Orphan Annie

Ah, at last I can plug my own publisher. *The Life and Hard Times of Little Orphan Annie* offers you the largest chunk of old waif dailies (Arlington, 1970). See also Dover's recent *Annie* paperback, which reprints two of the old Cupples & Leon compilations.

There are no easily available book-size collections of any of the other kid strips discussed in this chapter. *Annie Rooney* Sunday pages were reprinted in the McKay comic-book line of the thirties and forties, *Frankie Doodle* flourished in *Tip Top Comics* and a couple of one-shots. *Patsy* and *Dickie Dare* were reprinted in *Famous Funnies*. Graff's work, especially, suffered from the magazine's practice of relettering and whiting out all the tone patterns.

Chap. 9: MUSCLEMEN AND PALOOKAS

Joe Palooka

The champ showed up in *Famous Funnies, Feature Funnies, Big Shot Comics,* and a magazine of his own which lasted for several years.

Joe Jinks

Joe, and later Curly Kayoe, can be found in *Tip Top Comics.*

The Spirit

Eisner's rumpled mystery man is being reprinted in Warren's *Spirit* magazine. This is the Sunday sections, with only one story per issue in color. The daily strip is appearing in the *Menomonee Falls Gazette,* where the entire Jack Cole-ghosted sequence sampled here ran.

The Red Knight

America's least-known superhero has never been reprinted anywhere, except here. When I got permission to reprint the strip the Knight's own syndicate admitted even they'd never heard of him.

Miss Fury

The *Marvel Comics* folks reprinted Tarpe Mills's Sunday page in eight issues of a *Miss Fury* comic book in the early and middle forties. Sought after by both comic buffs and fetishists, the early issues sell for as high as $80.

Chap. 10: YOU BETCHUM!

Red Ryder

Red was in several comic books in the forties. Until recently the *Menomonee Falls Gazette* was reprinting some of Harman's uglier dailies.

The Lone Ranger

No book available of the masked man's newspaper adventures. Best source of the strip is the sundry comic books put out by the David McKay outfit in the 1930s and 1940s. The Ranger even appeared, for some reason, in a short-lived magazine called *Future Comics*.

King of the Royal Mounted

Sgt. King was reprinted in several issues of *Nostalgia Comics*.

Chap. 11: THE BOYS IN UNIFORM

Don Winslow

Once again you're limited to Don's various comic-book reprints (not to be confused with the original material put out by Fawcett in the forties). Anyone with further curiosity about Ken Ernst's version can also check the strips reprinted in *Comics & Their Creators* (Luna Press, 1971).

Roy Powers

Godwin's strips have been recently reprinted in Europe, but the only source in English remains the issues of *Famous Funnies* from thirty and more years ago.

* * * * * * * * * * * *

There are several dealers in comic strips around the country. At the moment there are two fanzines devoted to ads for runs of old strips. These are *Bull-Dog* (Box 368, Lynwood, Wash., 98036) and *The Stripper* (715 St. Marys, Decatur, Ind., 46733). *The Buyer's Guide*, a large bi-weekly tabloid, also gives space to ads from comic strip dealers (Dynapubs, address below).

* * * * * * * * * * * *

ADDRESSES

Dynapubs Enterprises
RR#1, Box 297
East Moline, Ill. 61244

   Publishers of *Vintage Funnies, The Buyer's Guide,* etc.
   Write for catalog.

House of Greystoke
6657 Locust St.
Kansas City, Mo. 64131

Luna Press
Box 1049
Brooklyn, N.Y. 11202

Menomonee Falls Gazette
Box 255
Menomonee Falls, Wis. 53051

Nostalgia Press, Inc.
Box 293
Franklin Square, N.Y. 11010

Overstreet's COMIC BOOK PRICE GUIDE
2905 Vista Dr. N.W.
Cleveland, Tenn, 37311

Acknowledgments
   I appreciate the co-operation of all the cartoonists and writers interviewed for this book. And I'd like to thank the following people for providing information, tear sheets, clippings, etc.: Jerry Bails, Orlando Busino, Dave Folkman, Jim Ivey, Gil Kane Peter Maresca, Richard Marschall, Tom Peoples, and Donald L. Puff.

Index

(Page numbers in italics indicate
illustrations of the strips listed)

220